A Student's Guide to SCANDINAVIAN AMERICAN Genealogy

Oryx American Family Tree Series

A Student's Guide to SCANDINAVIAN AMERICAN Genealogy

By Lisa Olson Paddock and
Carl Sokolnicki Rollyson

Oryx Press
1996

Copyright 1996 by The Rosen Publishing Group, Inc.
Published in 1996 by The Oryx Press
4041 North Central at Indian School Road
Phoenix, Arizona 85012-3397

Printed and bound in the United States of America

∞ The paper used in this publication meets the minimum
requirements of American National Standard for Information
Science—Permanence of Paper for Printed Library Materials,
ANSI Z39.48, 1984.

Library of Congress Cataloging-in-Publication Data
Paddock, Lisa Olson.
    A student's guide to Scandinavian American genealogy / Lisa
Olson Paddock, Carl Sokolnicki Rollyson.
        p.   cm. — (Oryx American family tree)
    Includes bibliographical references and index.
    ISBN 0-89774-978-2
    1. Scandinavian Americans—Genealogy—Handbooks, manuals, etc.
    2. Scandinavian Americans—Genealogy—Bibliography. I. Rollyson,
Carl Sokolnicki. II. Title. III. Series: Oryx American family tree.
E184.S18P33 1996
929'.1'089395—dc20   95-43086
                                                                CIP

Contents

The Swedish diplomat and businessman Raoul Wallenberg was captured by Russian troops because of his efforts to save Hungarian Jews from death camps during World War II. As a Scandinavian American, you can look back proudly on many Scandinavians and Scandinavian Americans who have fought for social justice and achieved distinction in a wide variety of fields.

Chapter 1
Tracing Your Roots

What do you say when someone asks you about your ethnic background? Do you immediately identify yourself as a Dane or a Norwegian? Or does your ethnic heritage resist such uncomplicated labels? Lisa Olson grew up in a family like the majority of contemporary American families: the product of a mixture of ethnicities. On her mother's side, she is the descendant of German and so-called Scotch-Irish immigrants who pioneered the American Midwest in the early nineteenth century. This part of her heritage seemed so thoroughly assimilated and distant in time as to have lost its ethnic coloration. On her father's side, in contrast, signs of her ethnic heritage were not at all hard to find: Her father's father was a Swede who had emigrated at the turn of the century as a boy. To this day she has vivid memories of her grandfather—whose speech was marked by a distinct Swedish accent all his life—singing Scandinavian songs to her when she was a small girl. Her ethnic identity was clear to her, as it was to her brothers: they were Swedish American.

Although she began to explore her Swedish American heritage at an early age, it wasn't until after her mother's death, by which time Lisa was an adult, that she recognized there was another side to her own history. Your own background, like hers, may reflect a mixture of ethnicities, and your current interest in your Scandinavian ancestry may be just the first step toward exploring a complex heritage.

Sooner or later most of us become curious about our roots. Perhaps a relative born in a foreign country is a member of the household, and his or her presence sparks an early interest in exploring where the family came from. Or perhaps the interest does not develop until after the death of an

1

important relative, when investigating the family's past becomes a significant way of honoring that person and preserving his or her memory. Perhaps a distant cousin visits for the first time and brings fascinating anecdotes about other relatives. Every family has stories to tell, adventures to be relived. Each generation treasures memories of a family's journey through life, but each also forgets. Searching for roots helps to preserve and even expand a family's story. And when people find out about their families they also discover aspects of themselves, details about what made them who they are.

You may have a specific reason for researching your family history. If you are adopted, you may want to find out about your birth parents. If your parents have died, you may be trying to learn more about them from other family members and friends. Or you may want to sort fact from fiction in the stories you have heard your parents and grandparents tell.

Unless a relative has become a family historian, you will probably learn that no one has all the facts. Even then, the picture will probably be less than complete. Lisa discovered after her mother died that late in life she had begun to assemble a kind of documentary ancestral history, consisting of photographs, letters, newspaper clippings, and the like. What was missing, however, was a narrative to bind these items together and explain their significance. Part of your job, like Lisa's, will be to reconstruct the family record. There are great rewards in store for you. You may be able, months or years from now, to present your family with its own unique story. Along the way, you will learn a great deal about Scandinavian and American history and the history of immigration. You will also become a practiced researcher—learning skills that will be useful for the rest of your academic and professional life.

If you are descended from Scandinavian immigrants, you are one of millions of people who helped to define the American identity. It may be that the street you live on, the park where you relax, or the school you attend has been named after a Dane, a Finn, an Icelander, a Norwegian, or a

Swede—a Scandinavian American who helped build this country. Learning about Scandinavia and Scandinavian Americans will mean discovering fascinating things about your neighbors and community, if not about your own family.

Scandinavian American Customs

When Scandinavians came to America, they did not leave their cultures behind them. In fact, immigrants found comfort by gathering with others of their heritage and practicing customs from their homeland. Some of these customs are still popular today in Scandinavian American communities, and many have caught on in mainstream America as well.

An ancient aspect of Finnish culture is the sauna, the hot mist bath now considered a chic form of relaxation in the United States. Traditionally Finnish men took a sauna together to calm their nerves and socialize. A long period in the 175°F steam was followed by a salty snack of sausages or preserved fish.

Fish still plays a major role in Scandinavian life. Immigrants' favorite types of fish and methods of preparation are an important contribution to U.S. cuisine. Salmon, one of the favorite fish of Scandinavia, is cooked in many ways: baked, boiled, broiled, stewed, smoked, dried, marinated, and grilled. Cod is particularly popular among Norwegians, who dry it, then soak it in lye before cooking it into a pungent dish called *lutefisk*.

The Danish are famed for their contributions to fine cheeses. Creamy white Havarti, sometimes flavored with fresh dillweed, is one of many distinctively Danish cheeses.

You have probably heard the Swedish word smorgasbord, meaning a big table groaning with food. This feasting table of hot and cold dishes was developed in Sweden in the late nineteenth century. It has become a favorite social event in Scandinavian communities in the United States. Many Swedish stick-to-the-ribs dishes are beloved in U.S. homes: Swedish meatballs mingled with sautéed onions and sour cream; Swedish pancakes topped with tart lingonberries.

The Christmas season is a good time to find evidence of Scandinavian traditions in the United States. It is customary in Scandinavia to have a lush green fir tree in the house at Christmas, as well as a pine Advent wreath. These used to be lit with real candles. Ornaments made of straw bound with ribbons, especially in the shape of goats, are a traditional Swedish craft still made in the United States. Several Scandinavian cultures have a special game for children at Christmas. Each child is given a bowl of sweet rice porridge; whoever finds the almond hidden in his or her porridge wins the prize: a marzipan pig. Santa Claus—the most identifiable symbol of Christmas for most American children—makes his home in Lapland, Finland's northernmost region.

Understanding Your Heritage

To understand the experiences of Scandinavian immigrants, you need to know something about the history of Scandinavia and about that part of it from which your ancestors came. The next chapter will provide a brief history of the "old country" and suggest further reading about Scandinavian culture and its outstanding figures.

Don't overlook the very rich tradition of the various Scandinavian literatures. The more you know about your parent country, the more you will discover what makes you both Scandinavian American and Danish, or Finnish, or Icelandic, or Norwegian, or Swedish. Your opinions about your family, community, and country may change as you explore the nature of what it means to be a Scandinavian American. You will probably become interested in comparing the experiences of Scandinavian Americans with those of other immigrant groups. This will be a research project that can be shared with friends, some of whom will doubtless be descendants of other immigrant groups. The **Resources** section at the end of this chapter introduces several books that provide insights into immigrant history, followed by sections specifically devoted to the separate histories of immigrants from Denmark, Finland, Norway, and Sweden.

You will also find sections concerning prominent

Eliel Saarinen was a Finnish American architect who contributed to the development of many American cities. Above, at the Architectural League Exhibition, Saarinen was awarded a gold medal in recognition of his work at the Cranbrook Institute.

Scandinavian Americans, such as the Saarinens, who arose from one of these separate, but similar groups. Eliel Saarinen (1873–1950) and Eero Saarinen (1910–1961) were a father and son team of Finnish American architects. The elder Saarinen first made a name for himself as the architect of the Helsinki, Finland, railway station, which was completed in 1914. After taking second prize in a prestigious architectural competition in Chicago in 1922, he took up residence in the United States, where his increasingly functional style had a profound effect on the development of several American cities, such as Detroit, where he headed the academy of art at the Cranbrook Institute. Among the influential buildings designed for public use by Eliel Saarinen are the Crow Island Elementary School in Winnetka, Illinois, and the music shed for the Berkshire Festival at Tanglewood, Massachusetts.

Eliel Saarinen's later projects were undertaken in

There may still be signs of Scandinavian influence in your community, even if establishments such as this Norwegian fish market in Brooklyn are a thing of the past.

conjunction with his son. Like his father, Eero Saarinen had a base in Detroit, where he was responsible for designing the innovative General Motors Technical Center. And like his father, Eero Saarinen also designed significant public buildings, such as American embassies in London and Oslo, the Trans World Airlines Terminal at Kennedy Airport in New York City, and the Dulles International Airport outside Washington, DC. Perhaps his greatest works are those at such prominent American universities as Yale, the University of Chicago, and the Massachusetts Institute of Technology.

Like much of the art created by Scandinavian Americans, the Saarinens' designs fuse Nordic romanticism with New World practicality, giving rise to a wholly new style that has come to seem quintessentially American. Because their work is seen and used daily by Americans who live, work, study, and travel through some of the nation's largest population centers and institutions of higher learning, they continue to shape the country's sensibilities.

You may be surprised to see how rapidly Scandinavian Americans adapted to their new land. They did, of course, experience setbacks and tragedies. Overcoming obstacles became part of the process of assimilating new experiences and adjusting to changes. The immigrant experience is a process of identity-formation. Immigrants have kept the United States a dynamic country, unwilling to be complacent, always in pursuit of new ways of doing things.

Scandinavian Americans constitute one of the major ancestry groups in the United States. This means that your family's history will be representative of the complex and diverse history of the United States. Your research may lead you to new photographs of relatives and of places where your family lived. You may see features resembling your own in a photo that is many years old. It will feel as if you are holding history in your hands—especially if the pictures mesh with the interviews, oral histories, and other tools that you will use to make the past live again.

The immigrant experience was a journey, a quest for a better life, a way to express oneself. Think of your research project as your own journey of self-expression. You can look back at the cumulative record of the past to see how your family history might have shaped your personality and family dynamics.

In the course of your research, you will learn how to read maps, secure various documents such as birth and death certificates and military records, and use a wide range of reference works. In public libraries and archives, in genealogical societies, and of course among members of your own family, you will find many people willing to help you. You will probably make mistakes. If this happens, remember that you can always backtrack. Do not be afraid to reinterview people and to reread materials. Veteran researchers will tell you that everyone goes through the same trial-and-error process. This book will give you many pointers on how to proceed and how to organize your research. Ultimately you will become more comfortable as you discover your own favorite ways of information-gathering.

Listed below are books and articles that will help you get started thinking about your roots and the place of Scandinavian Americans in the history of American immigration. Detailed information and more resources are listed in Chapter 3, Beginning Your Genealogical Search. For now, you might take inspiration from the stories of others. Read some of the autobiographies, oral histories, and historical and biographical studies recommended here. They will give you an idea of form, of what a genealogical study or family history can look like. These readings should give you the inspiration to go on; they will also provide you with working models.

Once you have a basic grounding in historical, biographical, and genealogical research—and after you master the basic history of your ancestral land—you will be able to create your own history and to act as your own guide to your Scandinavian American past, present, and future.

Resources

STARTING YOUR EXPLORATION

Bales, Carol Ann. *Tales of the Elders: A Memory Book of Men and Women Who Came to America as Immigrants, 1900–1930*. **Columbus, OH: Silver Burdett, 1993.**

Scandinavians were among the largest immigrant groups during the period that is the focus of this book. It recounts the stories of twelve men and women who journeyed to the United States during the period known as the Great Migration.

Lagerlöf, Selma. *The Changeling*. **New York: Knopf, 1992.**

A novel set in Sweden. A farmer's wife becomes the foster mother of a troll's child, and her humanistic treatment of the changeling eventually secures the return of her own son. Illustrated.

Martell, Hazel Mary. *Over 900 Years Ago: With the Vikings*. **Columbus, OH: Silver Burdett, 1993.**

Part of the "History Detective" series, this book examines the Vikings and their role in history as readers search for "clues." Illustrated with photographs and color artwork, such as time lines.

Newth, Mette. *The Abduction*. **Translated by Tina Nunnally and Steve Murray. New York: Farrar, Straus & Giroux, 1989.**

Translated from the Norwegian, this novel explores the experiences of the people who fell victim to Scandinavian voyages of discovery and conquest.

St. John, Betty. *A Family in Norway*. **Minneapolis: Lerner, 1988.**

The life of a Norwegian family is depicted in words and pictures.

Vitebsky, Piers. *Saami of Lapland.* **New York: Thomson Learning, 1994.**

The Saami live in the icy wilderness of northern Scandinavia. Reindeer herding and ice fishing support their vibrant culture, though their traditional way of life is increasingly endangered.

IMMIGRANT HISTORY

"America's Challenge." *Time,* **Special Issue, Fall 1993.**

A succinct history of immigration, the experiences of different ethnic groups, the changing attitudes of Americans toward immigration.

Appel, John J., ed. *The New Immigration.* **New York: Jerome S. Ozer, 1971.**

A collection of articles. See especially: "The Public School and the Immigrant Child," "The Second Generation of Immigrants in the Assimilative Process," and "European Peasants as Immigrants." Contains a chronology and bibliographical essay.

Bromwell, William J. *History of Immigration of the United States: Exhibiting the Number, Sex, Age, Occupation, and Country of Birth of Passengers Arriving from Foreign Countries By Sea, 1819–1855.* **New York: Augustus M. Kelley, 1969. [First published in 1856.]**

Tables of statistics. A separate section on laws relating to immigration and immigrants.

Crevecoeur, J. Hector St. John de. *Letters from an American Farmer.* **[First published in 1782.] New York: Dutton, 1957.**

See especially Chapter 3, "What Is an American?" Crevecoeur establishes the basic story of the immigrant, building America and working out of self-interest.

Handlin, Oscar. *The Uprooted: The Epic Story of the Great Migrations that Made the American People.* **Boston: Little, Brown, 1952.**

A classic of immigration history, with chapters on peasant origins, the crossing, new work in the New World, religious life, different generations of immigrants and their children, immigrant alienation from American life, restrictions on immigration, and the promise that the United States has held for generations of immigrants.

Neidle, Cecyle. *The New Americans.* **New York: Twayne Publishers, 1967.**

A concise history of American immigration from the colonial period to the 1930s, with excerpts from the writings of famous travelers to the United States, immigrants, immigrant leaders, political activists and politicians, union leaders, and professional writers. Bibliography.

Scott, Franklin D. *The Peopling of America: Perspectives on Immigration.* **Washington, DC: American Historical Association, 1972.**

Sections on migration history, the colonial period in North America, beginnings of the big surge (1783–1865), mass migrations (1865–1914). Bibliographical essay.

SCANDINAVIAN AMERICAN HISTORY: EXPLORATION, IMMIGRATION, AND SETTLEMENT

Abbott, Edith. *Immigration: Select Documents and Case Records.* **New York: Arno Press, 1969. [First published in 1924.]**

See index for Scandinavian case records. Some of these documents may be useful in your genealogical search.

Babcock, Kendric Charles. *The Scandinavian Element in the United States.* **New York: Arno Press, 1969. [First published in 1914.]**

Chapters on Swedes, Norwegians, and Danes, charting immigrant patterns, economic forces, religious and intellectual developments, social relations and characteristics, the Scandinavian in local politics, party preferences and political leadership. Critical essay on materials and authorities, statistical tables of populations, statistics of three Minnesota counties.

Bodnar, John. *The Transplanted: A History of Immigrants in Urban America.* **Bloomington: Indiana University Press, 1987.**

See index for references to Danes, Finns, and Swedes. Bodnar examines the unique experiences of immigrants in American cities. Although many Scandinavian Americans headed westward to states like Minnesota, a good number remained in eastern port cities like Boston and New York.

Carpenter, Niles. *Immigrants and Their Children 1920.* **Washington, DC: U.S. Government Printing Office, 1927.**

See index for references to Scandinavians.

Dinnerstein, Leonard; Nichols, Roger L.; and Reimers, David M. *Natives and Strangers: Ethnic Groups and the Building of America.* **New York: Oxford University Press, 1979.**

See index for references to Scandinavians, Finns, Norwegians, and Swedes.

Dinnerstein, Leonard, and Reimers, David M. *Ethnic Americans: A History of Immigration and Assimilation,* **2d ed. New York: Harper and Row, 1982.**

See index for references to Scandinavians, Danes, Finns, Norwegians, and Swedes.

Fairchild, Henry Pratt, ed. *Immigrant Backgrounds.* **New York: John Wiley & Sons, 1927.**

See Chapter 15, "The Scandinavians."

Friis, Erik J., ed. *The Scandinavian Presence in North America.* **New York: Harper's Magazine Press, 1973.**

Provides a statistical background as well as an examination of the church, the Augustana Church in the United States and in Sweden, Norwegian Lutheranism, Danish churches in America, brotherhoods and fraternal organizations, special-interest societies, education, the immigrant press, Scandinavia in books, the mother countries' respective assessments of Scandinavians in the United States.

Furer, Howard B., ed. *The Scandinavians in America 986–1970: A Chronology & Fact Book.* **Dobbs Ferry, NY: Oceana Publications, 1972.**

Detailed chronology, extensive list of documents, and bibliographies on Danish, Norwegian, and Swedish Americans.

Golab, Caroline. *Immigrant Destinations.* **Philadelphia: Temple University Press, 1977.**

See index for references to Norwegians and Swedes.

Greene, Victor. *A Passion for Polka: Old-Time Ethnic Music in America.* **Berkeley: University of California Press, 1992.**

See Chapter 9, "Americanized Scandinavian and Polish Bands: New York and the East, 1930–1960." Polka music was one of many Scandinavian contributions to the United States.

Hansen, Marcus Lee. *The Atlantic Migration: 1607–1860.* **Cambridge: Harvard University Press, 1940.**

A history from the colonial period to the Great Migration in the early twentieth century. Illustrations and bibliography. See index for references to Danes, Finns, Norwegians, and Swedes.

Kennedy, John F. *A Nation of Immigrants.* **New York: Harper & Row, 1964.**

A succinct overview. Appendixes on the chronology of immigration and suggested reading. See Chapter 4, "The Scandinavians."

Lieberson, Stanley. *Ethnic Patterns in American Cities.* **New York: The Free Press, 1963.**

Check index for references to Denmark, Finland, Norway, and Sweden.

———. *A Piece of the Pie: Black and White Immigrants Since 1880.* **Berkeley: University of California Press, 1980.**

See index for references to Danes, Finns, Norwegians, and Swedes. Lieberson's focus is the tension between African Americans and European immigrants caused by competition for jobs and other resources.

———, and Waters, Mary C. *From Many Strands: Ethnic and Racial Groups in Contemporary America.* **New York: Russell Sage Foundation, 1980.**

See index for references to Danes, Finns, Norwegians, and Swedes.

Liebman, Lance, ed. *Ethnic Relations in America.* **Englewood Cliffs, NJ: Prentice Hall, 1982.**

See index for references to Scandinavians.

Lowell, Briant Lindsay. *Scandinavian Exodus: Demography and Social Development of 19th-Century Rural Communities.* **Boulder: Westview Press, 1987.**

Chapters on the scale of the exodus, the causes of emigration, Swedish emigration 1881–1900, Norwegian emigration 1875–1905, comparison of Sweden to Norway. Bibliography.

Morrison, Joan, and Zabusky, Charlotte Fox. *American Mosaic: The Immigrant Experience in the Words of Those Who Lived It.* **Pittsburgh: University of Pittsburgh Press, 1993.**

See statements by Walter Lindstrom (Sweden), Anna Ohlson (Norway), Peter Kekkonen (Finland), Grete Rasmussen (Denmark), Liv Jorgensen (Norway).

Novotny, Ann. *Strangers at the Door: Ellis Island, Castle Garden, and the Great Immigration to America.* **New York: Viking Press, 1971.**

See index for references to Scandinavians, Danes, Finns, Norwegians, and Swedes.

Portes, Alejandro, and Rumbaut, Ruben G. *Immigrant America: A Portrait.* **Los Angeles: University of California Press, 1990.**

See index for references to Finns, Norwegians, and Swedes.

Ross, Edward Alsworth. *The Old World in the New: The Significance of Past and Present Immigration to the American People.* **New York: Century, 1914.**

See Chapter 4, "The Scandinavians."

Roucek, Joseph S., and Eisenberg, Bernard, eds. *America's Ethnic Politics.* **Westport, CT: Greenwood Press, 1982.**

See Chapter 16, "The Scandinavians."

Scott, Franklin D., ed. *Trans-Atlantica: Essays on Scandinavian Migration and Culture.* **New York: Arno Press, 1979.**

Essays on migration in the dynamics of history, the Great Migration from Europe, the dual heritage of the Scandinavian immigrant, literature in periodicals of protest of Swedish America, Swedish trade with America in 1820, cultural interchange in Scandinavia, Swedish students' images of the United States, American influences in Norway and Sweden, the causes and consequences of emigration in Sweden, the study of the effect of emigration, and other topics.

Skardal, Dorothy Burton. *The Divided Heart: Scandinavian Immigrant Experience through Literary Sources.* Lincoln: University of Nebraska Press, 1974.

Chapters on immigrant literature, English-language writers, emerging themes, motives for emigration, the voyage to and arrival in America, problems of adjustment, definitions of immigrant groups, attitudes toward American culture, the theme of success, social advancement, social classes, personality changes, educational opportunities, changes in immigrant institutions, cultural and social organizations, the press, politics, churches, changes in immigrant values (home and family), loss of European values, urban-rural ethics, the costs of success, folklore and folk music, old world festivals, problems of a dual heritage, World War I, bibliographies of Scandinavian American literature, index of Scandinavian immigrant authors.

Smith, William Carlson. *Americans in the Making.* New York: Arno Press, 1970. [First published in 1939.]

On the causes of immigration, the adjustments of immigrants to America (assimilation), the second generation, the immigrants' contributions to the United States. See index for specific references to Danes, Finns, Norwegians, Swedes, and Scandinavians. Bibliography.

Stephenson, George M. *A History of American Immigration 1820–1924.* New York: Ginn and Co., 1926.

See Chapter 3, "The Scandinavians."

Taylor, Philip. *The Distant Magnet: European Emigration to the U.S.A.* New York: Harper & Row, 1971.

See index for references to Danes, Finns, Norwegians, and Swedes.

Thernstrom, Stephan, ed. *Harvard Encyclopedia of American Ethnic Groups.* Cambridge: Harvard University Press, 1980.

Thematic essays on assimilation and pluralism, and on concepts of ethnicity, education, family patterns, immigration, literature and ethnicity; additional information on religions, resources, and research centers, and a survey of research. Individual entries on ethnic groups, including Danes, Finns, Norwegians, and Swedes. Maps, tables, and bibliography.

Vecoli, Rudolph J., and Sinke, Suzanne M. *A Century of European Migrations, 1830–1930.* **Urbana: University of Illinois Press, 1991.**

See Part One for an excellent overview of migration and immigration patterns. Chapters include: "Migration Traditions from Finland to North America," "Chain Migrations from the West Coast of Norway," and "A Pioneer Chicago Colony from Voss, Norway: Its Impact on Overseas Migration, 1836–60."

Wakin, Edward. *The Scandinavians in America.* **Chicago: Claretian Publications, 1974.**

Chapters on pioneers, Scandinavians in America, the trip westward, taking root.

SCANDINAVIAN AMERICAN LITERATURE

Bach, Giovanni. *The History of Scandinavian Literatures.* **New York: Dial, 1938.**

Includes Finnish and Icelandic literature. Extensive bibliographies and chapters on Danish American, Norwegian American, Finnish American, and Swedish American literature.

Di Pietro, Robert J., and Ifkovic, Edward. *Ethnic Perspectives in American Literature: Selected Essays on the European Contribution.* **New York: The Modern Language Association of America, 1983.**

See chapter on Scandinavian American literature.

HISTORY OF DANISH AMERICANS

Brunner, Edmund deSchweinitz. *Immigrant Farmers and Their Children.* Garden City, NY: Doubleday, Doran, 1929.

See the chapter titled "Askov: A Study of a Rural Colony of Danes in Minnesota."

Hvidt, Kristian. *Flight to America: The Social Background of 300,000 Danish Emigrants.* New York: Academic Press, 1975.

Chapters on mass emigration and public opinion, trends in the literature on the background and causes of mass emigration, Danish emigrants before they left, urban and rural emigration, emigration and internal migration, distribution of emigrants according to age, men and women among the emigrants, families and individuals during emigration, the occupations of emigrants, agricultural structure, emigration for political or religious reasons, Danish emigrants in the New World, return emigration. Bibliography.

DANISH AMERICAN LITERATURE

Mortensen, Enok. *Danish-American Life and Letters: A Bibliography.* Des Moines, IA: Committee on Publications of the Danish Evangelical Church in America, 1945.

Covers both Danish American literature and publications on the lives of Danish Americans.

NOTABLE DANISH AMERICANS

Jacob A. Riis (1849–1914)

Danish-born reformer, journalist, and author. He published several books on the poor in New York City, focusing on the poverty and squalor of living conditions for immigrants, especially in the tenements. His photographs provided powerful support for his campaign to improve living conditions for America's newest arrivals and the downtrodden.

Alland, Alexander. *Jacob A. Riis: Photographer & Citizen.* **Millerton, NY: Aperture, 1974.**

Photographs and bibliography.

Cordasco, Francesco, ed. *Jacob Riis Revisited: Poverty and Slum in Another Era.* **Garden City, NY: Doubleday, 1968.**

Illustrations.

Riis, Jacob A. *The Battle with the Slum.* **New York: Macmillan, 1902.**

Illustrations. A sequel to *How the Other Half Lives.*

————. *The Children of the Poor.* **New York: Scribner's, 1892.**

Photographs and diagrams.

————. *The Complete Photographic Work of Jacob A. Riis,* **edited by Robert J. Doherty. New York: Macmillan, 1981.**

A full collection of Riis's photos.

————. *How The Other Half Lives: Studies Among the Tenements of New York.* **New York: Scribner's, 1890.**

Photographs.

————. *The Making of an American.* **New York: Macmillan, 1901.**

Riis's autobiography. Illustrations.

————. *The Old Town.* **New York: Macmillan, 1909.**

About Ribe, Denmark, his birthplace, its social life and customs. Illustrations.

————. *A Ten Years' War: An Account of the Battle with the Slum in New York.* Freeport, NY: Books for Libraries Press, 1969. [First published in 1900.]

Sophus Keith Winthur
Winthur is noted for his realism and criticism of the American economy.

Winthur, Sophus Keith. *This Passion Never Dies.* New York: Macmillan, 1938.

> A novel about the harsh farm life of a Danish family in Nebraska.

HISTORY OF FINNISH AMERICANS

D'Innocenzo, Michael, and Sirefman, Josef P., eds. *Immigration and Ethnicity: American Society— "Melting Pot" or "Salad Bowl"?* Westport, CT: Greenwood Press, 1992.

> See "The Attenuated Ethnicity of Contemporary Finnish Americans."

Kivisto, Peter. *Immigrant Socialists in the United States.* Cranbury, NJ: Associated University Presses, 1984.

> Discusses the scholarship on immigrant radicalism, the Finnish background, the rise of the left, its successes and failures, its decline, the aftermath. Bibliography.

Ross, Carl, and Brown, K. Marianne Wargelin, eds. *Women Who Dared: The History of Finnish American Women.* St. Paul: Immigration History Research Center of the University of Minnesota, 1986.

> Essays on the history of Finnish American women, with a focus on rights and identity issues. Examples are drawn from women of diverse walks of life, from maids to ministers.

Turner, H. Haines. *Case Studies of Consumers' Cooperatives: Successful Cooperatives Started by Finnish Groups in the United States; Studies in Relation to Their Social and Economic Environment.* New York: Columbia University Press, 1941.

Geographical locations: Maynard, Massachusetts, and the Lake Superior region. List of tables, map.

Wargelin, John. *The Americanization of the Finns.* Hancock, MI: Finnish Lutheran Book Concern, 1924.

An examination of the assimilation process, as experienced by Finnish Americans.

FINNISH AMERICAN LITERATURE

Järvenpä, Aili. *Half Immersed and Other Poems.* St. Cloud, MN: North Star Press, 1978.

Poetry from a Finnish American perspective.

———, and Karni, Michaels, eds. *Sampo, The Magic Mill: A Collection of Finnish-American Writing.* Minneapolis: New Rivers Press, 1989.

A broad variety of short stories and poetry by Finnish Americans as well as translations of Finnish authors.

NOTABLE FINNISH AMERICANS

Eliel Saarinen (1875–1950) and Eero Saarinen (1910–1961)

Internationally acclaimed architects, born in Kirkkonummi, Finland. With his father, Eliel, Eero emigrated to the United States in 1923. He was educated at Yale, and then joined his father's architectural firm, building the University of Chicago law school, the Vivian Beaumont Theatre at New York City's Lincoln Center, and many other famous structures.

Christ-Janer, Albert. *Eliel Saarinen.* Chicago: University of Chicago Press, 1948.

Illustrations, plans, and bibliography.

Hall, Mildred Reed. *The Fourth Dimension in Architecture: The Impact of Building on Man's Behavior: Eero Saarinen's Administrative Center for Deere & Company, Moline, Illinois.* **Sante Fe: Sunstone Press, 1975.**

Illustrations.

Hausen, Marika. *Eliel Saarinen: Projects, 1896–1923.* **Cambridge: MIT Press, 1990.**

Illustrations and bibliography.

Kuhner, Robert A. *Eero Saarinen, His Life and Work.* **Monticello, IL: Council of Planning Librarians, 1975.**

Temko, Allan. *Eero Saarinen.* **New York: George Braziller, 1962.**

Illustrations and plans.

HISTORY OF NORWEGIAN AMERICANS

Andersen, Arlow W. *The Norwegian-Americans.* **Boston: Twayne, 1975.**

Chapters on Norway, the crossing and reception by Americans, the move westward, the pioneer press, Norwegian churches in the United States, public education and the church college, social and cultural organizations, and literature, leadership in business, the professions, and the arts, and relations between the United States and Norway. Notes and bibliography.

Bergmann, Leola. *Americans from Norway.* **Philadelphia: Lippincott, 1950.**

Chapters on Norway, emigration, Norwegians in Wisconsin, Iowa, Minnesota, the Red River Valley, the Dakotas, Montana, the Far West, the Pacific Northwest, and the Atlantic Coast. Separate sections on prairie society, the cities, sailors, and outstanding individuals. Bibliography.

Bjork, Kenneth O., ed. *Norwegian-American Studies.* **Northfield, MN: The Norwegian-American Historical Association, 1972.**

Articles on Norwegian soldiers in the Confederate forces during the American Civil War, Henrik Ibsen in Seattle, the 1842 immigrants from Norway, some recent publications, archives.

Blegen, Theodore. *Norwegian Immigration to America 1825–1860.* **New York: Arno Press, 1969. [First published in 1931.]**

The genesis of immigration, the spread of western settlement, rising emigration and westward expansion, emigration causes and controversy, the Norwegian government and early emigration, emigrant gold seekers, the Oleana colonization project in Pennsylvania, emigrant songs and poems, the eve of the Civil War. Illustrations and maps.

————, ed. *Norwegian-American Studies and Records.* **Northfield, MN: Norwegian-American Historical Association, 1940.**

Articles on Ibsen's *A Doll's House* in the United States, Scandinavian students at Illinois State University, Norwegian emigration to the United States during the nineteenth century, Ole Edvart Rölvaag biography, recent publications.

Curti, Merle. *The Making of an American Community: A Case Study of Democracy in a Frontier Community.* **Stanford: Stanford University Press, 1959.**

See index for references to Norwegian American settlements, reputation, occupations and economic status, land acquisition, farmers, political life, family names, intermarriage, acculturation, religion, literacy, education, and school attendance.

Gjerde, Jon. *From Peasants to Farmers: The Migration from Balestrand, Norway, to the Upper Middle West.* **Cambridge: Cambridge University Press, 1985.**

Tables, illustrations, and bibliography. See the preface for a discussion of the differences between the folklore and history of emigration.

Hillbrand, Percie V. *The Norwegians in America.* **Minneapolis: Lerner Publications, 1967.**

Chapters on geography and climate, early explorations of the Vikings, immigration in the nineteenth century, Norwegian settlements in the United States, contributions to American life and culture.

Ingwersen, Faith, and Norseng, Mary Kay, eds. *Fin(s) de Siecle in Scandinavian Perspective: Studies in Honor of Harald S. Naess.* **Columbia, SC: Camden House, 1993.**

Essays on the Norwegian American experience in Chicago.

Leiren, Terje. *Marcus Thrane: A Norwegian Radical in America.* **Northfield, MN: Norwegian-American Historical Association, 1987.**

A forceful and original pre-Marxist immigrant socialist, editor, reformer, playwright, and champion of the workingman's cause. Chapters on Thrane's European career, his becoming a Norwegian American, his career in the theater, his political agenda, and later years.

Lovoll, Odd S. *The Promise of America: A History of the Norwegian-American People.* **Minneapolis: University of Minnesota Press, 1984.**

Chapters on Norway and Europe, the emigration, the beginnings of Norwegian American society, the developing immigrant community, settling the land, religious life, the press and public life, cultural growth, the distribution of immigrants in rural and urban areas, Norwegian American organizations, the role of Norwegian Americans in American life, institutions, and their relationship to Norway. Illustrations and bibliography.

Munch, Helene, and Munch, Peter, eds. *The Strange American Way: Letters of Caja Munch from Wiota, Wisconsin, 1855–1859. With: An American Adventure, Excerpts from "Vita Mea," an Autobiography Written in 1903 for His Children by Johan Storm Munch.* **Carbondale: Southern Illinois University Press, 1970.**

Letters by a young woman, a newly married minister's wife, who accompanied her husband to the Middle West. Peter Munch's paternal grandfather, Johan, left a record of his life for his descendants. See the foreword for Peter Munch's discussion of his family history and how he put it together in this volume.

Norlie, Olaf Morgan. *History of the Norwegian People in America.* **New York: Haskell House, 1973. [First published in 1930.]**

Covers the history and literature of the new immigrants. Illustrations.

Pencak, William; Berrol, Selma; and Miller, Randall M., eds. *Immigration to New York.* **Philadelphia: Balch Institute Press, 1991.**

See especially "Mobilization and Conflict: The Background and History of the Norwegian Colony in Brooklyn to 1910."

Qualey, Carlton C. *Norwegian Settlement in the United States.* **New York: Arno Press, 1970. [First published in 1938.]**

Chapters on migration factors, the trip to Wisconsin, Iowa, North Dakota, Michigan, and the American West. Statistical tables and bibliography.

Semmingsen, Ingrid. *Norway to America: A History of the Migration.* **Minneapolis: University of Minnesota Press, 1978.**

Chapters on migration, pioneers, emigration, the United States in the 1850s, encountering Americans, politics and organizations, the immigrants becoming Americans, the emigrants and the homeland. Bibliography.

Skard, Sigmund. *The United States in Norwegian History.* **Westport, CT: Greenwood Press, 1976.**

Chapters on early explorations (1000–1500), the "Second Discovery" (1500–1750), the eighteenth century (1750–1807), as well as chapters on relationships between the United States and Scandinavian countries, the opening of the American continent (1815–1861), modern America (1861–1914), World War I and interwar period (1914–1940), and World War II and its aftermath. Bibliography.

Wheeler, Thomas C., ed. *The Immigrant Experience: The Anguish of Becoming American.* **New York: Dial Press, 1971.**

See Chapter 3, "Pioneers to Eternity: Norwegians on the Prairie."

NORWEGIAN AMERICAN LITERATURE

Waldemar Ager (1869–1941)
A historian and psychological novelist of immigrant life.

Ager, Waldemar. *Sons of the Old Country.* **Lincoln: University of Nebraska Press, 1983.**

Johan Bojer (1872–1959)
Writer of novels that vividly portray both the poverty of Norway and the harsh new world of Norwegian immigrants in the United States.

Bojer, Johan. *The Emigrants.* **New York: The Century Co., 1925.**

————. *The Everlasting Struggle.* **New York: The Century Co., 1931.**

————. *The Great Hunger.* **New York: Moffat, Yard & Co., 1919.**

——. *The Last of the Vikings*. New York: The Century Co., 1923.

Martha Ostenso (1900–1963)
A novelist of Norwegian American family life.

Ostenso, Martha. *Wild Geese*. New York: Dodd, Mead, 1925.

Ostenso's best-known work, set on the Manitoba prairie.

Ole Edvart Rölvaag (1876–1931)
One of America's most famous immigrant writers, Rölvaag created a major epic out of pioneer life and the settling of the country.

Boewe, Charles. "Rölvaag's America: An Immigrant Novelist's Views." *Western Humanities Review*, Vol. 11 (1957): 3–12.

An examination of Rölvaag's perspective on his adopted country.

Haugen, Einar. *Ole Edvart Rölvaag*. Boston: Twayne, 1983.

A friend of Rölvaag's, Haugen has written a fine introduction to his work, covering the major novels and including a biographical sketch, chronology, and annotated bibliography.

Rölvaag, Ole Edvart. *The Boat of Longing*. New York: Harper & Brothers, 1933.

Combines the mystical folktale and the realistic novel in the tragic story of immigration.

——. *Giants of the Earth: A Saga of the Prairie*. New York: Harper & Brothers, 1927.

The author's masterpiece, an epic saga of Norwegian immigrants building a life out of the wilderness.

——. *Peder Victorious*. New York: Harper & Brothers, 1929.

The sequel to *Giants of the Earth,* concentrating on Peder, the American-born child of immigrants, and on his ambitions.

————. *Their Father's God.* Lincoln: University of Nebraska Press, 1983. [First published in 1931.]

The author's last novel, a study of intermarriage between the Norwegians and the Irish.

Carrie Young

Young, a second-generation Norwegian American, has written several novels and a biography of her mother's emigration.

Young, Carrie. *Stories from the Dakota Plains.* **Iowa City: University of Iowa Press, 1992.**

Norwegian Americans in the Middle West during the 1930s. Illustrated.

NOTABLE NORWEGIAN AMERICANS

Thorstein Veblen (1857–1929)

An economist and social critic, Veblen was born to Norwegian immigrant parents and spent his first seventeen years in Norwegian American farm communities. A Yale Ph.D. who taught at the University of Chicago and other prestigious institutions, he was an original and controversial thinker, applying acute psychological analyses to social behavior and economic systems. He coined the term "conspicuous consumption." Several of his books have become classics, and he has become a much studied and emulated thinker.

Veblen, Thorstein. *Essays, Reviews, Reports: Previously Uncollected Writings.* **Joseph Dorfman, ed. Clifton, NJ: A. M. Kelley, 1973.**

This is a scholarly edition of many short published and unpublished works by the great economist.

————. *An Inquiry into the Nature of Peace and the Terms of Its Perpetuation.* **New York: Macmillan, 1917.**

Veblen wrote this tract in response to the outbreak of World War I. He applies his economic genius to the problem of keeping human society in balance to prevent future wars.

————. *The Theory of the Leisure Class*. Fairfield, NJ: A. M. Kelley, 1991.

This is Veblen's most famous book. His economic study of societal institutions considers why labor is divided up as it is in the western world.

HISTORY OF SWEDISH AMERICANS

Benson, Adolph B., and Hedin, Naboth. *Swedes in America 1638–1938*. New Haven: Yale University Press, 1938.

Articles on the Swedish language in the United States, farmers, pioneers, geographical distribution, Swedish place names in the United States, religion, charities and self-help, colleges, newspapers, writers in Swedish, magazines, authors, journalists, translations of Swedish literature, professors, public school educators, lawyers, public officials, doctors, gymnasts, sports figures, inventors, engineers, architects and builders, composers, opera singers, motion picture actors, stage and radio performers, painters and sculptors, soldiers and sailors, aviators, manufacturers, businessmen, imports and importers. Illustrations.

Dowie, Iverne, and Espelie, Ernest M., eds. *The Swedish Immigrant Community in Transition: Essays in Honor of Dr. Conrad Bergendoff*. Rock Island, IL: Augustana Historical Society, 1963.

Essays on the background of Swedish immigration (1840–1850), an immigrant community in central Kansas, the sacred music of Swedish immigrants, the academies of the Augustana Lutheran Church, the language of immigrants, the immigrant community during the Progressive era, the Swedish American press and isolationism, Conrad

Bergendoff (1918–1963), Christian scholar and educator. Maps, illustrations, and bibliography.

Erickson, Charlotte, ed. *Emigration from Europe 1815–1914: Select Documents.* **London: Adam & Charles Black, 1976.**

See Part 1, Chapter 4, and Part 2, Chapter 6 on Sweden and Swedish immigrants.

Holli, Melvin G., and Jones, Peter d'A. *The Ethnic Frontier: Essays in the History of Group Survival in Chicago and the Midwest.* **Grand Rapids, MI: William B. Eerdmans Publishing Co., 1977.**

See Chapter 4, " 'Becoming American': The Role of Ethnic Leaders—Swedes, Poles, Italians, Jews."

Janson, Florence Edith. *The Background of Swedish Immigration 1840–1930.* **New York: Arno Press, 1970. [First published in 1931.]**

Chapters on Sweden in 1840, on the landless agrarians, Swedish immigration to the United States in the 1840s, industrial Sweden, the passing of the old rural culture, and the Swedish industrial laborer. Bibliography.

Shenton, James P., and Brown, Gene. *Ethnic Groups in American Life.* **New York: Arno Press, 1978.**

See the index for references to Swedish Americans and Scandinavians.

Spengler, Paul A. *Yankee, Swedish, and Italian Acculturation and Economic Mobility in Jamestown, New York, from 1860 to 1920.* **New York: Arno Press, 1980.**

A comparison of the adjustment of different ethnic groups.

Stephenson, George M. *The Religious Aspects of Swedish Immigration.* **New York: Arno Press, 1969. [First published in 1932.]**

Chapters on the Church of Sweden, Baptists, Mormons, Methodists, the struggle for religious freedom, the Lutheran church, Episcopalians, and "Sweden and her American children in the twentieth century." Illustrations and bibliography.

Thomas, Dorothy Swaine. *Social and Economic Aspects of Swedish Population Movements 1750–1933.* **New York: Macmillan, 1941.**

See the index for references to emigration.

Wald, Arthur, ed. *American Swedish Handbook.* **Vol. III. Rock Island, IL: Augustana Book Concern, 1948.**

Articles on national organizations in the United States and Sweden, churches, colleges, publishers and booksellers, a century of Swedish immigration, Swedish stock in the United States, the Swedish American press, one hundred years of Swedish poetry in America, bibliographies.

SWEDISH AMERICAN LITERATURE

Bonggren, Jakob. *The Swedish Element in America.* **Chicago: University of Chicago Press, 1931.**

A discussion of Swedish culture and influence in the United States. See Volume II, "Swedish-American Literature," pp. 313–23.

Dahl, Borghild. *Karen.* **New York: Random House, 1947.**

Details the conflict between loyalty to the Swedish American family and assimilation into American life.

Kalm, Pehr. *The America of 1750: Peter Kalm's Travels in North America,* **2 vols. New York: Wilson-Erickson, 1937. [First published in 1770.]**

Describes both the United States and Canada.

Wright, Robert L. *Swedish Immigrant Ballads.* **Lincoln: University of Nebraska Press, 1965.**

Ballads in Swedish and English, with a bibliography and appendix of melodies.

NOTABLE SWEDISH AMERICANS

Henry M. Jackson (1912–1983)

A Democratic congressman and then senator from Washington, Jackson was a supporter of organized labor, civil rights, the migration of Soviet Jews, and a strong defense establishment. His efforts in 1972 and 1976 to secure the Democratic nomination for president were unsuccessful, although he had broad support not only from conservative and moderate Democrats but also from some Republicans, who admired his strong defense of the Vietnam War and other foreign policy positions.

Fosdick, Dorothy, ed. *Staying The Course: Henry M. Jackson and National Security*. Seattle: University of Washington Press, 1987.

An examination of Jackson's prodefense policies. Illustrations and bibliography.

Ognibene, Peter J. *Scoop: The Life and Politics of Henry M. Jackson*. New York: Stein and Day, 1975.

A relatively comprehensive biography of the late Senator.

Prochnau, William W. *A Certain Democrat: Senator Henry M. Jackson, A Political Biography*. Englewood Cliffs, NJ: Prentice-Hall, 1972.

A biography focusing on Jackson's political accomplishments. Illustrations.

Charles Lindbergh (1902–1974)

The Swedish American aviator who attained world renown by making the first west-to-east solo crossing of the Atlantic Ocean. His later life became controversial and tragic, when his child was kidnapped and killed, and he took a sympathetic attitude toward Hitler's Germany.

Mosley, Leonard. *Lindbergh: A Biography.* **Garden City, NY: Doubleday, 1976.**

Illustrations and bibliography.

Randolph, Blythe. *Charles Lindbergh.* **New York: Franklin Watts, 1990.**

Illustrations and bibliography. Covers both his early and later controversial life.

Chapter 2
Scandinavia, Scandinavians, and the History of Immigration

Scandinavians are not a homogeneous people. There is an old Scandinavian joke, retold in Edward Wakin's *The Scandinavians in America* (Chicago: Claretian Publications, 1974), that illustrates some of the stereotypical differences:

> [T]wo Danes, two Norwegians, two Finns, and two Swedes were shipwrecked on a desert island. By the time they were rescued, the Danes had formed a cooperative, the Norwegians had built a fishing vessel, the Finns had chopped down all the trees, and the Swedes were still waiting to be introduced. (p. 41)

But while there certainly are major differences among the four peoples, it is also true that they have common ethnic, cultural, and—except for the Finns, whose language does not have Indo-European roots—linguistic origins. Their political histories are often intertwined. Norway was a part of first Denmark, then Sweden; and Finland was a Swedish province for much of its early history. The Kalmar Union, starting in 1397 and lasting for more than a century, consolidated Denmark, Norway, and Sweden under one sovereign.

Periodic attempts have been made to renew such solidarity. "Scandinavianism" was revived during the mid-nineteenth century, when notions of a common Nordic ancestry were kindled by the spirit of romanticism that swept through Europe, sustained by fears of German and Russian imperialism. In 1853, at the outset of the Crimean War, during which Great Britain and France fought Russia, Denmark joined with what was then Sweden-Norway in a neutrality

In 1638, Swedes established a successful colony on the banks of the Delaware River.

pact, a pattern that would be repeated, with variations, during World War I. And in 1953, Sweden, Denmark, Norway, and Iceland inaugurated a political and cultural consultative body, the Nordic Union, which Finland joined in 1955.

As might be expected, the reasons for the emigration of Danes, Finns, Norwegians, Swedes, and—in far fewer numbers—Icelanders to America both differed and shared common elements. Interaction with the rest of the world came early with the voyages of the Vikings. Starting at the end of the eighth century, the Vikings made inroads into what is now Great Britain and Ireland, culminating in the acceptance, in 1016, of Cnut, son of Sweyn Forkbeard, the Danish conqueror, as undisputed king of all England. Around the same time, the Danes established a dominion in Normandy, on the northern coast of France, and the Viking influence would be felt in England once more in 1066 with the Norman conquest. Six centuries later, when the English colonized America, they carried their Viking heritage with them.

In 1638, just eighteen years after the *Mayflower* landed on Plymouth Rock, a group of Swedes set up a successful colony along the banks of the Delaware River. But the founders of the New Sweden colony may not have been the first Scandinavians to set foot on American soil. The earliest written record of the discovery of the American mainland dates from 1070, but exploration of the eastern coast of North America probably came earlier.

Starting in the second half of the ninth century, the Norwegians settled Iceland. In the 980s, Erik the Red, a Norwegian exile, was banished from Iceland and began exploring Greenland to the west, where he established two colonies. In about the year 1000, his son, Leif, sailed to "Markland," which was probably somewhere on Labrador Island, and continued south to an area he called "Vinland," which legend equates with the area we know as New England. Whether or not Leif Eriksson succeeded in establishing a colony in Newfoundland or actually landed in America is still an open question—muddied by propaganda disseminated by overeager Scandinavian immigrants like Johan Alfred Enander, who proclaimed in 1892, "the first European to set foot on American soil was not an Italian, but a Scandinavian."[1]

Nineteenth-Century Immigration

By the mid-1800s, most of Europe was experiencing an unusually large population growth. Finland's population, for example, tripled between 1750 and 1850. In the Scandinavian countries, unlike much of the rest of Europe, urban centers did not change as fast as did the countryside during this period. To keep such a large population economically viable, small farmlands were consolidated. Owners

---

[1] Edward Wakin, *The Scandinavians in America* (Chicago: Claretian Publications, 1974).

Scandinavian Americans were among the largest groups of immigrants to the United States for almost 100 years. Many headed immediately to the midwestern states, taking advantage of farmland that had been scarce in their home countries.

and tenants of smaller plots had to find other ways to make a living. This change caused a huge increase in the landless class. Many of these disenfranchised people became share-croppers and struggled against poverty. Meanwhile the rich elite became richer. Even village common lands came under their ownership. The landless could no longer use these lands for grazing their livestock or gathering lumber. People were forced to take wage jobs, and eventually many moved to urban areas in search of employment.

The Scandinavian governments reacted to this situation by encouraging emigration. The United States was painted in the public mind as a land of milk and honey. Hans Christian Andersen summed up popular feeling in an 1836 poem:

> Ducks and chickens raining down,
> Geese land on the table,
> Forks are out, the bird's done brown.
> Eat now if you're able.

Oh no! Can it be so true?
Is there so much joy for you?
A pity that America
Lies off so very far.[2]

In the late 1840s and early '50s the news of gold discoveries in California reached Scandinavian ears. Not many could afford so long a journey. Most of those who made it to California were seamen who jumped ship in San Francisco. Nevertheless, the few who went inspired others. The Gold Rush turned out to be the start of mass emigration to the United States.

Meanwhile, Scandinavians had been trickling into the American Midwest for twenty years. By the 1830s enclaves of Swedes and Norwegian Quakers already existed in Wisconsin, Minnesota, and Illinois. These communities served as beacons of welcome to new immigrants. The Danish influx gathered speed in the 1850s. Many had been converted in Denmark to the Mormon faith. It is estimated that about half of the Danes who came here in that decade did so to follow their new Mormon beliefs.

In the 1860s the Quincy Mining Co. in Michigan spread the word that it was seeking miners to emigrate from Finland and work for them. Quincy was short of help because many of its men had gone to fight in the Civil War. This news was greeted with joy in Finland, where many men had recently been laid off from the mines at Kafjord.

Iceland was the last to follow. Although it had suffered years of sheep epidemic and poor fish harvests, it did not receive information about the United States as quickly as did other Scandinavian countries. Serious emigration from Iceland did not begin until the 1870s.

The great majority of Scandinavian immigrants worked as farmers, as they had in Europe. They moved to areas where

---

[2] Hans Norman and Harald Runblom, *Transatlantic Connections: Nordic Migrations to the New World after 1800* (Oslo: Norwegian University Press, 1982).

This engraving depicts the Norwegian explorer Leif Eriksson sighting the American coast. It is believed that he landed near Labrador Island and traveled as far south as present-day New England.

vast lands lay to be cultivated if one was willing to work extremely hard and risk all one had. Homesteaders traveled to the Midwestern states, staking out cheap land in exchange for a promise to grow something on it. Under the provisions of the 1862 Homestead Act, homesteaders were required to cultivate their land within a certain time or forfeit their right to it. For this reason, Scandinavian immigrant farmers chose crops that would turn a fast profit. For example, many Norwegians grew tobacco, something they had never grown in their homeland. The Danish took a different approach. Using traditional skills, they focused on animal products. They flourished in the business of processing ham and bacon, and applied their expert management techniques to the first cooperative dairies in the United States.

When the Scandinavians began to immigrate to the United States in earnest in the mid-1800s, they were not strangers to the new land. But the ease with which they settled in had less to do with forerunners like Leif Eriksson and the settlers of the New Sweden colony than with their ethnicity and temperament. The majority of Scandinavian immigrants to America came from Norway and Sweden, which lost approximately one-quarter and one-third, respectively, of their total populations between the 1820s and the outbreak of World War I. After the Irish, Norwegians and Swedes constituted the largest group of immigrants to the United States during this period. But unlike some other immigrant groups—say, the Irish or the Poles—the Scandinavians were not set apart by their devotion to religion or fierce dedication to nationalism in their home countries. Indeed, some Norwegians and Swedes came to America to escape the dogmatism of their state-controlled Lutheran churches.

The assimilation of Scandinavian immigrants was also speeded by their immediate withdrawal to the hinterlands. Unlike many other immigrant groups, they did not settle next to competing groups in the crowded cities of the eastern seaboard. Instead, they took a direct route—sometimes even in marching columns headed by flag bearers—to the upper Midwest, to latitudes and landscapes nearly identical to those they had left behind.

Scandinavians were, in the main, drawn to the United States by the promise of land. Their native countries all had shortages of arable land, and this scarcity became an urgent matter when famines followed in the wake of a series of poor harvests during the period 1850–1880. As early as 1825, a group of Norwegian Quakers came over on the Scandinavian version of the *Mayflower, The Restauration*, but continuous Norwegian migration did not begin until the 1840s. The Swedes followed in the 1850s, as did the Finns. Migration for both groups peaked in the 1880s, when they were joined by the Danes and some Icelanders. The Danes, blessed with proportionately more farmland, and the Icelanders, afflicted with fewer economic pressures, came in far fewer numbers, and Icelandic immigration came to a full stop around the turn of the century.

A statue in New York's Battery Park commemorates John Ericsson, a Swedish engineer who designed the victorious Civil War ironclad warship, the *Monitor*.

The passengers on *The Restauration* set a pattern that would be followed by most subsequent Scandinavian immigrants. They traveled up the Hudson River by steamboat from New York City to Albany, where they transferred to canal boats that took them up the Erie Canal to Buffalo. There they boarded the Great Lakes boats that carried them to railheads in midwestern cities like Chicago, from which they dispersed to smaller settlements, mainly in Illinois, Iowa, Minnesota, Wisconsin, and the Dakotas.

The Scandinavian immigrants were so numerous and such valued customers that steamship companies, railroads, and even states competed for their business. In their native countries, prospective emigrants could purchase tickets that would take them anywhere in the United States. They were met when they arrived in the United States by agents of the emigrant companies that had arranged their transport. The railroads that carried them inland offered special rates. An 1881 advertisement for the St. Paul, Minneapolis & Manitoba Railroad read: "The settler—his family, household

The Danish-born journalist Jacob Riis exposed the horrific working conditions of many immigrants in New York City in the early 1900s.

goods, livestock and agricultural implements—will be carried from St. Paul to any point on either of our lines at one-half the regular price."

Once they arrived at their destinations, most of them began farming. They also immediately capitalized on one of their major attributes, their literacy (illiteracy had been virtually eliminated in Norway, Sweden, and Denmark by the nineteenth century), starting newspapers and—above all—schools. Many of these schools were connected with the Lutheran church, but the Scandinavian immigrants were also staunch supporters of the public school system, where their children could learn English. There were differences among ethnic groups, of course. The Swedes remained more closely bound to the church. The Finns had greater difficulty assimilating because they had to surmount a greater linguistic barrier. In the main, however, they all made a quick, easy transition to life in their new country.

By the time of the Civil War (1861–1865), Scandinavians were a part of the American fabric. Almost without exception, they sided with the Union. One out of every six Scandinavians fought with the Union Army, and a Swedish engineer, John Ericsson, was responsible for designing the Union warship *Monitor*, which defeated the Confederate ironclad *Merrimack*, assuring Union naval superiority and making Ericsson an American hero.

World War I (1914–1918) made travel to America hazardous, and immigration quotas, first imposed in 1921, cut back further on the number of Scandinavians emigrating to the United States. Still, between 1820 and the outbreak of World War I, 2 million Scandinavians came to the United States. Today, the number of Americans of Scandinavian ancestry is over 10 million. Over time, their occupations, like those of the rest of the nation, became industrialized, their locations urbanized. Today, although Scandinavian ethnic groups are diffused, certain areas still retain a Scandinavian flavor: Minneapolis and New York have the greatest concentrations of Norwegians, more Swedes live in Chicago than in any other urban area, Los Angeles is home to the largest

Dag Hammarskjöld, a Swede, served as secretary general of the United Nations for eight years and was actively involved in efforts to bring peace to the Middle East in the 1950s.

number of city-dwelling Danes, and the majority of Finnish Americans reside in Michigan.

Assimilation and Accomplishment

By settling mainly in the Midwest and making themselves a part of the "heart of the heart of the country" at a time when the nation was still expanding, Scandinavian immigrants quickly became an integral part of the United States. Their cultural and ethnic ties with the larger, dominant population of descendants of British ancestry—together with their eagerness to learn English—facilitated their assimilation. Their success has come at some cost; ethnic awareness and facility in their ancestral languages among third- and fourth-generation Scandinavian Americans have declined as Scandinavian population centers have decreased in size and number. But Scandinavians have distinguished themselves in countless fields of endeavor: the secretary general of the United Nations Dag Hammarskjöld, the pioneering journalist Jacob Riis, the economist and social critic Thorstein Veblen, the glamorous film star Greta Garbo, and the heroic aviator Charles Lindbergh are only a few of the personages who help to illustrate the breadth of Scandinavian and Scandinavian American achievement.

Scandinavian and Scandinavian American women have made their mark in many fields. Women who have served in Scandinavian government include Denmark's minister of economy, Marianne Jelved; Finland's minister of defense, Elisabeth Rehn; Iceland's minister of social affairs, Johanna Sigurdardottir; Iceland's president, Vigdis Finnbogadottir; Norway's minister of agriculture, Gunhild Oyangen; Norway's prime minister, Gro Harlem Brundtland; and Sweden's foreign minister, Margaretha af Ugglas. Icelandic-born poet Kristjana Gunnars, Norwegian-born writer Brenda Ueland, and Finnish American actress Christine Lahti are just a few of the many Scandinavian American women who have shared their talents with the world.

Resources

SCANDINAVIAN HISTORY

Arneson, Ben A. *The Democratic Monarchies of Scandinavia*. New York: Van Nostrand, 1949.

Chapters on the land and the people, political history, policymaking, administration of justice, local government, labor problems, social legislation. Bibliographical note.

Butler, Ewan. *The Horizon Concise History of Scandinavia*. New York: American Heritage Publishing Co., 1973.

Chapters on the Ice and Iron ages, Middle Ages, Royal Union and peasant separatism, Sweden's rise, reformation and religious wars, age of absolutism, eighteenth-century enlightenment, joining the continental system. Includes Denmark, Finland, Norway, and Sweden. Illustrations and chronology.

Connery, Donald S. *The Scandinavians*. New York: Simon and Schuster, 1966.

Part 1 is a history of Scandinavia, its traditions, culture, and government. The subsequent parts focus on individual countries. Bibliography.

Derry, T. K. *A History of Scandinavia: Norway, Sweden, Denmark, Finland and Iceland*. Minneapolis: University of Minneapolis Press, 1979.

From the Stone and Bronze Ages, the Vikings, early Christendom, early efforts at Scandinavian unity, the Lutheran kingdoms, monarchies, the impact of European wars, regionalism, Scandinavia in the nineteenth century, to the impact of World Wars I and II. Parallel table of events, notes, bibliography, maps.

Du Chaillu, Paul B. *The Land of the Midnight Sun: Summer and Winter Journeys Through Sweden, Norway, Lapland, and Northern Finland,* 2 vols. **New York: Harper & Brothers, 1881.**

An account of journeys made between 1871 and 1878. A study of Scandinavian peoples, their land, manners, and customs. Also based on research into prehistoric and Viking periods and the work of Norwegian and Swedish archaeologists. Maps and 235 illustrations.

Elazar, Daniel J.; Liberles, Adina Weiss; and Werner, Simcha. *The Jewish Communities of Scandinavia.* **Lanham, MD: University Press of America, 1984.**

Includes an overview and separate chapters on Sweden, Denmark, Norway, and Finland. Notes and glossary of Hebrew terms.

Franck, Harry A. *A Scandinavian Summer: Impressions of Five Months in Denmark, Finland, Sweden, Norway, and Iceland.* **New York: Century, 1930.**

Illustrations. A wide-ranging travel narrative, covering both urban and rural settings. Even though this book is quite old, it may help you to imagine what your ancestors' lives were like.

Friis, Henning, ed. *Scandinavia: Between East and West.* **Ithaca: Cornell University Press, 1950.**

Essays on Scandinavian democracy, Scandinavia in a changing world economy, government economic planning and control, the labor movement, social welfare, housing, producer and consumer cooperatives, adult education, foreign policy, cooperation among Scandinavian countries, the United States and Scandinavia. Statistical appendix and bibliography. Dated but interesting reading.

Fullerton, Brian, and Williams, Alan F. *Scandinavia: An Introductory Geography.* **New York: Praeger, 1972.**

Includes Denmark, Southern Jutland, Western and Northern Jutland, Central and Eastern Jutland, Sweden, Finland, Norway. Chapters on climate and vegetation, historical, social and economic background, international trade and relations. Bibliography.

Griffiths, Tony. *Scandinavia.* **South Australia: Wakefield Press, 1991.**

A lively, succinct modern history of the Scandinavian nations.

Ingstad, Helge. *Westward to Vinland: The Discovery of Pre-Columbian Norse House-Sites in North America.* **New York: St. Martin's Press, 1969.**

Early explorations of North America by the Greenlanders, Vikings, and other Nordic peoples. Illustrations, notes, and bibliography.

Innes, Hammond. *Scandinavia.* **New York: Time Inc., 1963.**

Chapters on Scandinavian kingdoms of the North, the Viking Age, the urbane Danes, industrious Swedes, culture and climate. An appendix with historical dates and bibliography. Illustrations.

Maarbjerg, John P. *Scandinavia in European World Economy, ca. 1570–1625: Some Local Evidence of Economic Integration.* **New York: Peter Land, 1995.**

Focuses on Funnen-Langeland in Denmark and East Bothnia in Finland in a study of local response to economic integration.

Ogrizek, Dore, ed. *Scandinavia.* **New York: McGraw Hill, 1952.**

Chapters on Denmark, Norway, Sweden, Finland, and Iceland. Separate chapters on the art and literature of Scandinavia.

Taylor, Bayard. *Northern Travel: Summer and Winter Pictures: Sweden, Denmark, and Lapland.* **New York: Putnam's, 1883.**

A travel diary. Read the observations of a traveler to Scandinavia more than one hundred years ago.

Wuorinen, John H. *Scandinavia.* **Englewood Cliffs, NJ: Prentice-Hall, 1965.**

A survey of twentieth-century Scandinavia, the lands and peoples, history, governments, World Wars I and II, post-war economic patterns, Iceland, foreign policy trends, Scandinavian unity and cooperation. Bibliography and maps.

MEDIEVAL SCANDINAVIA AND THE VIKINGS

Bekker-Nielsen, Hans, et al. *Mediaeval Scandinavia.* **Odense: Odense University Press, 1971.**

Essays on the old Icelandic literary tradition, several medieval works of literature, a Norse-Celtic bibliographical survey.

Davidson, H. R. Ellis. *Pagan Scandinavia.* **New York: Praeger, 1967.**

Chapters on religion, farming communities and families, warfare. Photographs, line drawings, map, bibliography.

Foote, Peter G., and Wilson, David M. *The Viking Achievement: A Survey of the Society and Culture of Early Medieval Scandinavia.* **New York: Praeger, 1970.**

Includes Denmark, Sweden, Norway, and Iceland. Chapters on slaves and the free, Christianity and paganism, women and marriage, authority and administration, daily life, trade and towns, transport, warfare, art and ornament, poetry, justice, religion and conduct. Maps and bibliography.

Graham, Campbell, and Kidd, Dafydd. *The Vikings.* **New York: Morrow, 1980.**

Chapters on the Scandinavian background, ships and the sea, traders and looters, Viking settlements, house and home, death and the pagan gods, Viking dress, kings and coinage, Viking crafts, the coming of Christianity. Bibliography and illustrations.

Jones, Gwyn. *A History of the Vikings.* **New York: Oxford University Press, 1968.**

Chapters on the legendary history of Swedes and Danes, the Viking kingdoms, the Viking movement overseas, the ending of the Viking age. Illustrations and bibliography.

MacCulloch, J. A. *The Celtic and Scandinavian Religions.* **London: Hutchinson's, 1948.**

A separate section on Scandinavia, exploring myths, Scandinavian deities, lesser supernatural beings, nature and beings derived from it, worship, magic and divination, the Scandinavian universe, the future life, the fate of the gods and of the world.

Magnussen, Magnus. *Vikings!* **New York: Dutton, 1980.**

Chapters on mythology and history, Norway and Denmark after the first Viking raids, Danish invasions of England, Iceland, Greenland, and Vinland (North America), the end of the Viking age. Bibliography and illustrations.

Oxenstierna, Eric. *The Norsemen.* **Greenwich, CT: New York Graphic Society Publishers, 1965.**

Chapters on the Viking character, raids, forays into Russia, the Orient, North America, the Viking heritage. Maps, glossary, illustrations, and bibliography.

Poertner, Rudolf. *The Vikings: Rise and Fall of the Norse Sea Kings.* **New York: St. Martin's Press, 1971.**

Chapters on the early Viking raids, voyages to Vinland (North America), clan organization, peasant kings, sea kings, Viking warfare and statecraft, trade, conversion to Christianity. Chronology, illustrations, maps, bibliography, a "tourist guide to the Vikings" (a listing of sites). Look to see whether your ancestral village may once have been in Viking country.

Roesdahl, Else, and Wilson, David M., eds. *From Viking to Crusader: The Scandinavians and Europe 800–1200.* **New York: Rizzoli, 1992.**

Chapters on Scandinavia and Europe, culture and society, artifacts and manuscripts. Beautifully illustrated with maps, chronological table, bibliography, indiexes of places and objects, maps.

Sawyer, P. H. *The Age of the Vikings,* **2d ed. New York: St. Martin's Press, 1971.**

Chapters on the written sources, archaeology, the ships, treasure, raids, Danish settlements, towns and trade. Illustrations and bibliography.

Simpson, Jacquelin. *The Viking World.* **New York: St. Martin's Press, 1980.**

Chapters on the Viking character (ruffians or heroes?), life on land, ships and seafaring, merchants, weapons and warriors, family and society, games, art and poetry, religious practices and funerary rites. Bibliography and illustrations.

TWENTIETH-CENTURY SCANDINAVIA

Allardt, Erik, et al. *Nordic Democracy: Ideas, Issues, and Institutions in Politics, Economy, Education, Social and Cultural Affairs of Denmark, Finland, Iceland, Norway, and Sweden.* **Copenhagen: Det Danske Selskab, 1981.**

Scandinavia is often admired for its stable democracies and strong economies, although the Swedish and Finnish economies have recently been under strain. See especially Chapter 31: "Nordic Cultural Cooperation with the World at Large." Bibliography.

Anderson, Stanley V. *The Nordic Council: A Study of Scandinavian Regionalism.* **Seattle: University of Washington Press, 1967.**

The Nordic Council, founded in 1952, is an official consultative assembly of members of the parliaments of Denmark, Finland, Iceland, Norway, and Sweden. Anderson traces its history, its organization, its policies and actions, and the development of a Nordic market. Bibliography.

Elting, John R. *World War II: Battles for Scandinavia.* **New York: Time Life, 1981.**

Several picture essays on Sweden, Norway, and battles in Scandinavia. Bibliography.

John, Brian. *Scandinavia: A New Geography.* **New York: Longman, 1984.**

Part I: The Scandinavian environment (geography and culture, including Sweden, Denmark, Finland, Norway, and Iceland); Part II: Spatial expressions of human economy (farming, mining, manufacturing, service industries, rural and urban settlements); Part III: Regional inequalities (the heartland vs. the fringe, Lapland); Part IV: Local landscapes and sample studies (small communities); Part V: Unity and stress (cultural cooperation, regional development, environmental factors).Bibliography.

Nissen, Henrik S., ed. *Scandinavia During the Second World War.* **Minneapolis: University of Minnesota Press, 1983.**

Essays on the Nordic societies, German domination, resistance movements, the adjustment to allied victory, Nordic security policy after the war. Bibliographical note.

Scott, Franklin D. *Scandinavia.* **Cambridge: Harvard University Press, 1975.**

Includes Finland and Iceland as Scandinavian countries. See especially Chapter 6, "Scandinavian-American Crosscurrents." Bibliography and statistical appendix.

Shirer, William L. *The Challenge of Scandinavia: Norway, Sweden, Denmark and Finland in Our Time.* **Boston: Little Brown, 1955.**

Lengthy chapters on each country based on the distinguished journalist's travels and research. With an introduction covering initial observations, a capsule of geography, the bonds between Scandinavian peoples, their history of neutrality, occupation during World War II, and Scandinavia and the United States.

Sundelius, Bengt. *Foreign Polices of Northern Europe.* Boulder, CO: Westview Press, 1982.

Essays on the Nordic region and twentieth-century politics, economics, and how Nordic policies affect developing countries. Bibliography.

Turner, Barry. *The Other European Community: Integration and Cooperation in Nordic Europe.* New York: St. Martin's Press, 1982.

Contemporary economic history focused on Scandinavia, Denmark, Norway, Finland, and Iceland. Also a chapter on social democracy in Scandinavia. Illustrations and bibliography.

SCANDINAVIAN LITERATURE

Bredsdorff, Elias; Mortensen, Brita; and Popperwell, Ronald. *An Introduction to Scandinavian Literature: From the Earliest Time to Our Day.* Cambridge: Cambridge University Press, 1951.

Discusses Danish, Swedish, and Norwegian literature.

***Five Modern Scandinavian Plays.* New York: Twayne, 1971.**

C. E. Soya, *Lion with Corset*; W. Chorell, *The Sisters*; D. Stefansson, *The Golden Gate*; N. Grieg, *Our Power and Our Glory*; P. Lagerkvist, *The Man Who Lived His Life Over*.

Gustafson, Alrik, ed. *Six Scandinavian Novelists: Lie, Jacobsen, Heidenstam, Selma Lagerlöf, Hamsun, Sigrid Undset.* Princeton: Princeton University Press, 1940.

Essays on each novelist, with an introduction by the editor discussing the importance and the influence of Scandinavian fiction.

Leach, Henry Goddard, ed. *A Pageant of Old Scandinavia*. **Princeton: Princeton University Press, 1946.**

Chapters on old Scandinavian literature (epics and myths), legendary heroes, Iceland, Norway, Greenland, Denmark, Sweden. Bibliography.

Mawby, Janet. *Writers and Politics in Modern Scandinavia*. **London: Hodder & Stoughton, 1978.**

Concentrates on the twentieth century, especially the World War II period (1939–1945). Bibliography.

Modern Scandinavian Plays. **New York: Liveright, 1954.**

Plays by August Strindberg, Kaj Munk (Danish), Tryggvi Sveinbjornsson (Icelandic), Trygve Kielland (Norwegian).

Rossel, Sven H. *A History of Scandinavian Literature: 1870–1980*. **Minneapolis: University of Minnesota Press, 1982.**

Includes chapters on Icelandic and Nordic literature, and a chapter on recent trends in Scandinavian literature. Bibliography.

Seymour-Smith, Martin. *Guide to Modern World Literature*. **London: Macmillan, 1986.**

See chapter on Scandinavian literature.

Topsoe-Jensen, H. G. *Scandinavian Literature: From Brandes to Our Day*. **New York: W. W. Norton, 1929.**

Excludes Finnish literature. Chapters on the modern awakening, naturalism, Neo-Romanticism and Symbolism, and New Currents 1900–1914. A selected list of Scandinavian books and index of authors.

HISTORY OF DENMARK

Denmark: An Official Handbook. Copenhagen: Royal Danish Ministry of Foreign Affairs, 1974.

Chapters on the monarchy, land and people, prehistory, history, language, the constitution, government and administration, foreign affairs, domestic affairs, the judicial system, religion, defense, education, public finance, social security, family planning, health services, housing and planning, transport and communications, mass communications, trade and industry, manpower and employment, living standards, environment and conservation, science, research, technology, the arts, sport and games, bibliography. Illustrations.

Johansen, Hans Christian. *The Danish Economy in the Twentieth Century*. New York: St. Martin's Press, 1987.

Chapters on trends in economic and social development, peace and war, Denmark during World War II, the welfare state. See the introduction for a comparison of nineteenth- and twentieth-century Denmark. Bibliography.

Miller, Kenneth E. *Denmark*. Santa Barbara, CA: Clio Press, 1987.

Annotated bibliography of introductory works (older and recent descriptions, picture books, books for children); geography (maps and atlases, glossaries, Denmark as a part of Scandinavia, environment, tourism and travel); prehistory, archaeology and ethnography, history, population, religion, society, politics and government, foreign relations, economy, trade, industry, transport, agriculture and forestry, employment and labor, statistics, education, science and technology, languages, literature, the arts, music and dance, theater and film, sports and recreation, libraries, archives and museums, books and the media, periodicals and newspapers, encyclopedias. Map.

Oakley, Stewart. *A Short History of Denmark*. New York: Praeger, 1972.

> Chapters on earliest inhabitants, the early Middle Ages, the age of the Valdemars, decay and renewal, Scandinavian union, religious upheaval, the ages of Christian IV, Frederik III, and the end of the seventeenth century, the eighteenth century, the nineteenth century and Romanticism, the foundations of modern Denmark, the two world wars, and Denmark since 1945. Bibliography and illustrations.

Randsborg, Klavs. *The Viking Age in Denmark: The Formation of a State*. New York: St. Martin's Press, 1980.

> Chapters on the Vikings and the state, historical sources, runestones, people in a changing society, subsistence and rural settlement, towns and fortresses. Illustrations, notes, bibliography, index of place names and subjects.

TWENTIETH-CENTURY DENMARK

Flender, Harold. *Rescue in Denmark*. New York: Simon and Schuster, 1963.

> Covers the occupation of Denmark, persecution of the Jews, their flight and rescue, and the aftermath in Sweden and Denmark. Illustrations.

Goldberger, Leo, ed. *The Rescue of the Danish Jews: Moral Courage under Stress*. New York: New York University Press, 1987.

> Essays on Danish Jews in concentration camps and efforts to help Jews during the German occupation of Denmark. A section of personal narratives. Illustrations.

Meyer, Niels L.; Petersen, K. Helveg; and Sorensen, Villy. *Revolt from the Center*. Boston: Marion Boyars, 1981.

> An analysis of the democratic center political parties and

political action in Denmark. Chapters on political change and how to accomplish an ecologically sustainable society. Bibliography.

DANISH LITERATURE

Hans Christian Andersen (1805–1875)

A staple of children's literature because of his fairy tales, Andersen was also a travel writer whose work was read throughout Europe and the United States.

Andersen, Hans Christian. *The Story of My Life.* **Boston: Houghton Mifflin, 1871.**

> A detailed account of Andersen's life and work to the year 1867.

Bredsdorff, Elias, ed. *Eighty Fairy Tales/Hans Christian Andersen.* **New York: Pantheon Books, 1982.**

> Includes the well-known tales as well as less familiar ones such as "The Gardener and the Squire," "The Story of a Mother," "In a Thousand Years' Time," and "The Shadow."

———. *Hans Christian Andersen: The Story of His Life and Work, 1805–1875.* **New York: Scribner's, 1975.**

> A scholarly, comprehensive biography. See the preface for an excellent analysis of earlier treatments of Andersen's life and work. Illustrations and bibliography.

Conroy, Patricia L., and Rossel, Sven H. *The Diaries of Hans Christian Andersen.* **Seattle: University of Washington Press, 1990.**

> Chapters on his early years, travels in Europe, old age, and last years. Bibliography.

Spink, Reginald. *Hans Christian Andersen and His World.* **New York: Putnam, 1972.**

> A short, copiously illustrated biography, with a separate chronology of Andersen's life.

Stirling, Monica. *The Wild Swan: The Life and Times of Hans Christian Andersen.* **New York: Harcourt, Brace & World, 1965.**

A splendid, graceful biography. See the evocative first chapter, "Seasons in Copenhagen." Bibliography.

Herman Bang (1857–1912)

A novelist and short story writer, praised for his naturalistic style.

Bang, Herman. *Denied a Country.* **New York: Knopf, 1927.**

Set in a small Danish frontier town, the novel centers on a homeless violin virtuoso and is representative of Bang's spare, dramatic, and impressionistic style.

———. *Tina.* **Dover, NH: Athlone Press, 1984.**

Set on the southern Danish island of Als, Bang's birthplace, at the time of the Schleswig war of 1864. Tina is a servant girl who succumbs to the passions of war.

Anders Bodelsen (1937–)

Distinguished for his superb handling of both psychological and mystery stories.

Bodelsen, Anders. *Freezing Down.* **New York: Harper & Row, 1971.**

A science-fiction novel involving characters who have been frozen and thawed several times.

———. *Think of a Number.* **New York: Harper & Row, 1969.**

A thriller.

Cecil Bodker (1927–)

A writer of fables and mystical literature.

Bodker, Cecil. *The Leopard.* **New York, Atheneum, 1975.**

An Ethiopian boy finds his life endangered when he discovers that a disguised blacksmith, not a leopard, is responsible for a great many missing cattle in the area.

———. *Silas and Ben-Godik*. New York: Delacorte, 1973.

Silas and his friend Ben-Godik spend a year traveling by horseback and encountering many strange individuals and harrowing adventures.

Isak Dinesen (1885–1962)

The most celebrated author of modern Danish literature, a master of the short story and essay forms, Dinesen is often lauded for her gothic imagination and sensitive depictions of her travels.

Dinesen, Isak. *Anecdotes of Destiny*. New York: Random House, 1958.

The lighter side of Dinesen.

———. *Ehrengard*. New York: Random House, 1963.

Critic Robert Langbaum calls it a "comic masterpiece."

———. *Out of Africa*. New York: Random House, 1938.

Draws on Dineson's experiences living on a coffee plantation in Kenya from 1914 to 1931.

———. *Shadows on the Grass*. New York: Random House, 1961.

Autobiographical reminiscence, a continuation of *Out of Africa*.

Hannah, Donald. *Isak Dinesen and Karen Blixen: The Mask and the Reality*. New York: Random House, 1971.

Explores both the early years and the African phase, the function of her imagination, her religious themes. Bibliography.

Henriksen, Aage. *Isak Dinesen/Karen Blixen: The Work and the Life.* **New York: St. Martin's Press, 1988.**

A biographical/critical study emphasizing Dinesen's place in modern European literature and her mature fiction.

Thurman, Judith. *Isak Dinesen: The Life of a Storyteller.* **New York: St. Martin's Press, 1982.**

The best biography, covering the entire range of Dinesen's life and work. Illustrations and bibliography.

Meir Goldschmidt (1819–1897)

A novelist, dramatist, and journalist who struggled to be accepted into the mainstream of Danish literature and found himself ostracized because he was a Jew.

Ober, Kenneth H. *Meir Goldschmidt.* **Boston: Twayne, 1976.**

Chronology, biographical sketch, notes, and bibliography. An introductory study.

Søren Kierkegaard (1813–1855)

One of the great figures of modern philosophy and literature, usually associated with the development of existentialism, which Kierkegaard defined as a radical separation between God and man and the inexplicability or absurdity of the relations between them. Much of modern drama, often called the "Theater of the Absurd," draws on his ideas as well as the earlier realistic dramas of Ibsen.

Kierkegaard, Søren. *A Kierkegaard Anthology.* **New York: Modern Library, 1946.**

A collection of Kierkegaard's writings.

———. *Selections from the Writings of Kierkegaard.* **Garden City, NY: Doubleday, 1960.**

A sampling of Kierkegaard's work.

Kaj Munk (1889–1944)

The most important modern Danish playwright, whose themes deal with the conflict between power and love, and the yearning for a strong hero.

Munk, Kaj. *Five Plays*. New York: American-Scandinavian Foundation, 1953.

Get a taste for Munk's style with these five selections.

Klaus Rifbjerg (1931–)

A figure in what has been called the "lyrical blossoming" of postwar Danish poetry, Rifbjerg has also written major novels, stories, scripts, and films.

Rifbjerg, Klaus. *Anna, I, Anna*. Willimantic, CT: Curbstone Press, 1982.

A diplomat's wife abandons her comfortable life for an on-the-road adventure with a hippie.

Villy Sorensen (1929–)

A central figure in the intellectual life of postwar Denmark, Sorensen has been influenced by Isak Dinesen, Thomas Mann, and Franz Kafka. He tends to combine surrealistic and ironic attitudes with both realistic and mythical stories.

Sorensen, Villy. *The Downfall of the Gods*. Lincoln: University of Nebraska Press, 1989.

Illustrations.

———. *Tutelary Tales*. Lincoln: University of Nebraska Press, 1988.

A collection of Sorensen's short stories.

HISTORY OF FINLAND

Hall, Wendy. *Green Gold and Granite: A Background to Finland*. London: Max Parrish, 1953.

Divided into three parts: "A Land and a People," "A

People and Its Achievements," and "The State and the Nations." Separate chapters on Sibelius and *Kalevala*. Bibliography, Finnish and Swedish place names, and notes on Finnish pronunciation.

Jutikkala, Eino. *A History of Finland*. New York: Praeger, 1962.

Chapters on the settlement of the country, its place in the Western cultural sphere, in the Scandinavian union, the Middle Ages to the modern period, Finland as part of a great power, its relationships with Sweden and Russia, as an autonomous state, its loss and recovery of independence. Maps.

Nickels, Sylvie; Kallas, Hillar; and Friedman, Philippa, eds. *Finland: An Introduction*. New York: Praeger, 1973.

Chapters on Finnish history, independence, communism, rural life, industry and foreign trade, waterways, cities, wilderness, wildlife and nature, military, language, the church, architecture, design, literature, music (Sibelius), painting and sculpture, theater, food, Finns abroad. Includes useful addresses, bibliography, statistics, and illustrations.

Olin, S. C. *Finlandia: The Racial Composition, the Language, and a Brief History of the Finnish People*. Hancock, MI: The Book of Concern, 1957.

Chapters on the people, the Viking age in Finland, agriculture, industry, education, literature, music and art, religion. Illustrations, charts, tables, maps, bibliography.

Screen, J. E. O. *Finland*. Santa Barbara, CA: Clio Press, 1981.

Annotated bibliography on introductory works (older and recent descriptions, picture books, books for children); geography (maps and atlases, glossaries, Finland as part of Scandinavia, environment, tourism and travel); prehistory, archaeology and ethnography, history, population, religion, society, politics and government, foreign relations, economy, trade, industry, transport, agriculture and forestry, employment and labor, statistics, education, science and technology, languages, literature, the arts, music and dance, theater and film, sports and recreation, libraries, archives and museums, books and the media, periodicals and newspapers, encyclopedias. Map.

Shearman, Hugh. *Finland: The Adventures of a Small Power.* **New York: Praeger, 1950.**

Finland's history, domination by Sweden and Russia, its pro-German sympathies in World War I, social conditions, nationalism, industrialism, independence, civil war, external relations, economy, the war with Russia preceding World War II. List of important events in Finnish history.

Singleton, Fred. *A Short History of Finland.* **Cambridge: Cambridge University Press, 1989.**

Chapters on the land and the people; Finland, Sweden, and Russia in the eighteenth century; the Finnish national awakening; the Finnish economy in the nineteenth century; the political development of the country 1863–1917; independent Finland; Finland in World War II and postwar periods; its economy in the twentieth century; aspects of national identity, family life, social services, sport, literature, the church. Bibliography and appendix with copies of important historical documents.

Stoddard, Theodore Lothrop. *Area Handbook for Finland.* **Washington, DC: The American University, 1974.**

Country summary (vital statistics), chapters on history and character of the country, its political, economic, and military development. Illustrations, tables, glossary, and bibliography.

Vloyantes, John. P. *Silk Glove Hegemony: Finnish-Soviet Relations, 1944–1975: A Case Study of the Theory of the Soft Sphere of Influence.* **Kent, OH: Kent State University Press, 1975.**

"Silk glove" refers to the fact that the Soviet Union decided on a soft sphere of influence in Finland after World War II—that is, the Soviet Union chose not to occupy or annex the country but rather make sure that Finland's policies coincided with Soviet aims. This policy in Finland was used as an argument that the Soviet Union aimed not at taking over Western Europe but at a "Finlandization" of it.

TWENTIETH-CENTURY FINLAND

The Finnish Blue Book: The Development of Finnish-Soviet Relations during the Autumn of 1939 Including the Official Documents and the Peace Treaty of March 12, 1940. **Philadelphia: Lippincott, 1940.**

A collection of documents with an introduction and maps.

Gripenberg, G. A. *Finland and the Great Powers: Memoirs of a Diplomat.* **Lincoln: University of Nebraska Press, 1965.**

An inside account of the events leading up to the "winter war" between Finland and the Soviet Union. Chronology and bibliography.

Jakobson, Max. *Finnish Neutrality: A Study of Finnish Foreign Policy Since the Second World War.* **New York: Praeger, 1968.**

Chapters on Finnish history (1917–1944) and the postwar development of neutrality. Finland has always had to balance its affinity with the other Nordic countries with the might of its powerful eastern neighbor, Russia.

Rautkallio, Hannu. *Finland and the Holocaust: The Rescue of Finland's Jews.* **New York: Holocaust Library, 1987.**

The effects of Nazi racial policy in Finland (1938–1939), the arrival of Jewish refugees (1938), the treatment of refugees. Bibliography.

Wuorinen, John H., ed. *Finland and World War II 1939–1944.* **Westport, CT: Greenwood Press, 1983. [First published in 1948.]**

Chapters on Finnish foreign policy between the two world wars, Finland's foreign policy 1938–1939, on the eve of the war, the winter war and peace on March 12, 1940, Finland under the Moscow peace, Finland and the war 1941–1944. Maps and documents.

FINNISH MUSIC

Jean Sibelius (1865–1957)

Greatly revered in Scandinavia, Sibelius has a worldwide reputation. He had a great affinity for the countryside and Finnish legends, especially the epic *Kalevala*, which he expressed in a series of tone poems and in seven symphonies produced between 1898 and 1924.

Abraham, Gerald, ed. *The Music of Sibelius.* **New York: Da Capo Press, 1975.**

Essays on the man, his symphonies, miscellaneous orchestral and theater music, chamber music, piano music, songs, choral music, and the special characteristics of his style. Chronology, bibliography, indexed list of compositions, musical examples.

Ekman, Karl. *Jean Sibelius: His Life and Personality.* **Westport, CT: Greenwood Press, 1972. [First published in 1938.]**

Chapters on his parentage, happy childhood, musical education, life in Helsinki, his Norwegian friends, his last winter of study, his artist's life in Vienna, productive years, his work as a composer and teacher, his development in the last years of the nineteenth century, World War I, the civil war in Finland, his musical achievement. Includes a list of his works, illustrations, and a bibliography.

James, Burnett. *The Music of Jean Sibelius.* **Madison: Fairleigh Dickinson University Press, 1983.**

Chapters on Sibelius the man, separate chapters on his major symphonies. Also a chapter on Sibelius and the theater. Bibliography, recommended recordings, index of Sibelius's works.

Layton, Robert. *Sibelius.* **London: J. M. Dent, 1978.**

Chapters on the composer's early years, his major symphonies, other orchestral music, choral music, songs, chamber and instrumental music, Sibelius and the piano, his reputation and stature. Appendixes include a catalog of works and a bibliography.

FINNISH LITERATURE

Bosley, Keith, trans. *The Kalevala.* **Oxford: Oxford University Press, 1989.**

A recent translation by an award-winning British poet.

Dauenhauer, Richard, and Binham, Philip, eds. *Snow in May: An Anthology of Finnish Writing, 1945–1972.* **Rutherford, NJ: Fairleigh Dickinson University Press, 1978.**

A collection of work by Finnish writers. Bibliography.

Hawkins, H., and Lehtonen, S., eds. *On the Border: An Anthology of New Finnish Writing.* **Manchester, U.K.: Carcanet Press, 1995.**

Read what Finland's newest literary voices are saying.

Kalevala: The Land of Heroes, **2 vols. New York: Dutton, 1907.**

Finland's national epic. Introduction, brief summary of the poem's structure, notes, glossary of Finnish names.

Rubulis, Aleksis. *Baltic Literature: A Survey of Finn-*

ish, Estonian, Latvian, and Lithuanian Literatures.
Notre Dame, IN: University of Notre Dame Press,
1970.

Includes Finnish texts in translation and history and criticism of the literatures. Bibliography.

Schoolfield, George C., ed. *Swedo-Finnish Short Stories.* **New York: Twayne, 1974.**

Stories by Sara Wacklin, Joohan Ludvig Runeberg, Zacharias Topelius, John Hedberg, Jac Ahrenberg, Jonathan Reuter, Karl August Tavastsjerna, Guss Mattsson, Gustav Alm, Runar Schildt, Hans Ruin, Jarl Hemmer, Hagar Olsson, Elmer Diktonius, Rabbe Enckell, Titoi Colliander, Solveig von Schoultz, Mirjam Tuominen, Lorenz von Numbers, Ralf Parland, Hans Fors, Anders Cleve, Johan Bargum. Includes an introduction.

Simonsuuri, Kirsti, ed. and trans. *Enchanted Beasts: Modern Women Poets in Finland.* **London: Forrest Books, 1990.**

Translations of poetry by eleven Finnish poets, along with introductions to their work.

Bo Carpelan (1926–)
Perhaps the greatest contemporary Finnish poet. Praised for his concise style and lyrical beauty.

Carpelan, Bo. *Bow Island: The Story of a Summer That Was Different.* **New York: Delacorte Press, 1971.**

An eleven-year-old boy learns a great deal about human relationships during a summer spent on an island in the Baltic Sea.

———. *Room without Walls: Selected Poems.* **Boston: Forest Books, 1987.**

Includes an introduction.

Tove Jansson (1914–)

Author of a series of children's books about the Mumin trolls, popular with adult readers as well, since they parallel the world of the Swedo-Finnish upper class.

Jansson, Tove. *Comet in Moominland*. New York: H. Z. Walck, 1959.

Illustrations. In this first novel (published in Finland in 1947), Moomintroll encounters a mouth-organist, a moth collector, and a lovely maiden and discovers the danger of a threatening comet when he takes a journey to seek advice from the Professor.

Aleksis Kivi (1834–1872)

A novelist who writes about southern Finland.

Kivi, Aleksis. *Seven Brothers*. New York: American-Scandinavian Foundation, 1962.

Has been read as a simple tale of adventure by Finns of all ages, but it can also be read as a "key to the Finnish character."

Hagar Olsson (1893–1978)

Attacks contemporary problems in Finland.

Olsson, Hagar. *The Woodcarver and Death*. Madison: University of Wisconsin Press, 1965.

In this novel Olsson presents a poem about country life with mystical overtones.

J. L. Runeberg (1804–1877)

The undisputed poet of his nation, even though his language is Swedish. He is the product of a bilingual culture, sometimes referred to as Swedo-Finnish or Finlandic. See the introductory study by Tore Wreto, *J. L. Runeberg*. Boston: Twayne, 1980.

Runeberg, J. L. *The Tales of Ensign Stal*. New York: American-Scandinavian Foundation, 1960.

Runeberg's most popular and enduring work, set in the early nineteenth century and recounting the heroic Finnish resistance to the Russian invasion of 1808.

Henrik Tikkanen (1924–)
Controversial for his attacks on the Swedish upper class.

Tikkanen, Henrik. *The Thirty Years War*. Lincoln: University of Nebraska Press, 1987.

Illustrations. This novel centers on a Finnish soldier who refuses to accept his defeat in the Finnish-Russian war of 1940. A satirical, fast-paced antiwar protest.

HISTORY OF ICELAND

Bararson, Hjalmar Rognvaldur. *Iceland: A Portrait of Its Land and People*. Reykjavik: H. R. Bararson, 1982.

This native of Iceland has written a loving history and description of his land and culture. Illustrated with photos by the author.

Johannesson, Jon. *A History of the Old Icelandic Commonwealth*. Winnipeg: University of Manitoba Press, 1974.

A good book for an introduction to Iceland and how it functioned in premodern Europe.

Nordal, Sigurur. *Icelandic Culture*. Ithaca, NY: Cornell University Library, 1990.

This V. T. Bjarnar translation of *Islenzk Menning* tells of the development of Iceland to 1262, using old Norse literature and modern commentary.

ICELANDIC LITERATURE

Bachman, W. Bryant, Jr. *Four Old Icelandic Sagas and Other Tales*. Lanham, MD: University Press of America, 1985.

Sagas are narratives describing heroic deeds. Most were recorded in the twelfth and thirteenth centuries. Featured tales in this book include the Saga of Clever Ref, the Story of Thorstein of the East Fjords, and the Saga of the Oathbound Men.

Magnusson, Sigurur A., and Gunnars, Kristjana, eds. *Icelandic Writing Today*. Reykjavik: Icelandic Writing Today, 1982.

The editors interviewed more than a dozen Icelandic writers about their methods of working and their sense of nationality. Examples of their work supplement the text.

Mitchell, Philip Marshall, and Ober, Kenneth H. *Bibliography of Modern Icelandic Literature in Translation*. Ithaca: Cornell University Press, 1975.

This volume will refer you to translated works by modern Icelandic writers.

HISTORY OF NORWAY

Derry, T. K. *A History of Modern Norway 1814–1972*. Oxford: Clarendon Press, 1973.

A comprehensive look at many aspects of Norwegian history, such as the economy, government, nationalism, and Norway's experiences in various wars. Maps, notes, and bibliographical essay on books in English.

Hodne, Fritz. *The Norwegian Economy 1920–1980*. New York: St. Martin's Press, 1983.

Chapters on labor conflicts, investment, growth and stagnation, crises and cartels, market forces, government, and the economy. See especially the editor's introduction for a comparison of nineteenth- and twentieth-century Norway. Bibliography.

Sather, Leland B. *Norway*. Santa Barbara, CA: Clio Press, 1986.

Annotated bibliography on introductory works (older and recent descriptions, picture books, books for children), geography (maps and atlases, glossaries, Norway as part of Scandinavia, environment, tourism and travel), prehistory, archaeology and ethnography, history, population, religion, society, politics and government, foreign relations, economy, trade, industry, transport, agriculture and forestry, employment and labor, statistics, education, science and technology, languages, literature, the arts, music and dance, theater and film, sports and recreation, libraries, archives and museums, books and the media, periodicals and newspapers, encyclopedias. Map.

Storing, James. *Norwegian Democracy*. Boston: Houghton Mifflin, 1963.

Chapters on the land and the people, the government (the king and Council of State), national administration, political parties, courts, local government, social security system, the state and the economy, and Norway in the world community. Map, bibliography, and appendix with Norway's constitution.

TWENTIETH-CENTURY NORWAY

Arntzen, Jon Gunnar, and Knudsen, Bard Bredrup. *Political Life and Institutions in Norway*. Oslo: University of Oslo, 1981.

A study of government on the national, regional, and local levels. Bibliography.

Burgess, Philip M. *Elite Images and Foreign Policy Outcomes: A Study of Norway*. Columbus: Ohio State University Press, 1967.

Deals with World War II and the postwar period. Bibliography.

Eckstein, Harry. *Division and Cohesion in Democracy: A Study of Norway*. Princeton: Princeton University Press, 1966.

Chapters on Norway as a democracy, its political divisions, sense of community, social authority patterns. Tables and appendix on a theory of stable democracy.

Petrow, Richard. *The Bitter Years: The Invasion and Occupation of Denmark and Norway, April 1940–May 1945*. New York: Morrow, 1974.

Chapters on Scandinavian neutrality, the invasions of Denmark and Norway, occupied Denmark, the rescue of the Danish Jews, victory in Denmark and Norway. Bibliography.

Ramsoy, Natalie Rogoff, ed. *Norwegian Society*. New York: Humanities Press, 1974.

Chapters on population, family, kinship and marriage, the economy, education, political institutions, religion, the health system, mass media, leisure, administration of justice, Norway in the world community. Bibliography, name and subject index.

NORWEGIAN ART

Edvard Munch (1862–1944)

One of the most prolific modern artists, Munch created 1,008 paintings, as well as drawings, watercolors, engravings, and sculptures. He came from an old Norwegian family of considerable distinction. Evidence of his traumatic childhood appears in his art. He is perhaps best known for a series of paintings titled *The Scream*.

Deknatel, Frederick B. *Edvard Munch*. New York: Chanticleer Press, 1950.

The catalog of an exhibition with biographical narratives, notes on the text, illustrations, and bibliography.

Heller, Reinhold. *Munch: His Life and Work*. Chicago: University of Chicago Press, 1984.

Chapters on his childhood and youth, artistic beginnings, years of indecision, formation of a new aesthetic, his period in Berlin, years of crisis and success. Notes, illustrations, and bibliography.

Messer, Thomas M. *Edvard Munch.* **New York: Abrams, n.d.**

Oversize collection of reproductions in color, with a biographical outline and selected bibliography.

NORWEGIAN LITERATURE

Beyer, Harald. *A History of Norwegian Literature.* **New York: New York University Press, 1956.**

Chapters on antiquity and the Vikings, the sagas, ballads and folktales, the Reformation and humanism, Ludvig Holberg, Ibsen, Bjornson, realism, Hamsun and Kinck, Sigrid Undset. Guide to pronouncing Norwegian names, bibliography, index of names and titles.

Hanson, Katherine, ed. *An Everyday Story: Norwegian Women's Fiction.* **Seattle, WA: The Seal Press, 1984.**

Introduction on the role of women in Norwegian literature. Thirty stories comprise the first anthology of prose fiction by Norwegian women writers to appear in English translation.

Jorgenson, Theodore. *History of Norwegian Literature.* **New York: Haskell House, 1970. [First published 1939.]**

Covers the earliest poetry (runes, eddic poems, skalds), medieval literature, folk literature, humanism and Reformation, Holberg and his age, romanticism, Ibsen, Bjornson, realism, naturalism, neo-romanticism and symbolism, neo-realism, contemporary currents.

Tryggve Andersen (1866–1920)

One of Norway's greatest short story writers, influenced by Edgar Allan Poe.

Andersen, Tryggve. *In the Days of the Councillor*. New York: Twayne, 1969.

> A novel set in eighteenth-century Norway, focusing on the interaction between educated civil servants and traditional farmers.

Johan Borgen (1902–1979)
One of the most inventive stylists of the 1930s.

Borgen, Johan. *Lillelord: A Novel*. New York: New Directions, 1982.

> About a little boy, Wilfred Sagen, from the secure middle-class world of Oslo. Absorbing portrayal of mother and son.

Olav Duun (1876–1939)
Writes in the dialect of his native village on the island of Joa, concentrating on everyday lives.

Duun, Olav. *The People of Juvik: A Saga of Modern Norway*. New York: Knopf, 1930–1935.

> Six volumes. The story of a peasant family over a hundred-year period up to the end of World War I. The background of the series is four centuries of history.

Johan Falkberget (1879–1967)
Portrays the struggle for existence among workers and mountain peasants in northern Norway.

Falkberget, Johan. *The Fourth Night Watch*. Madison: University of Wisconsin Press, 1968.

> A novel set in a nineteenth-cnetury mining town. The introduction explains the novel's role as social commentary.

Knut Hamsun (1859–1952)
One of the great writers of modern literature, hailed by Thomas Mann, Isaac Bashevis Singer, and others, for using

his subjectivity, lyricism, flashbacks, and other themes and techniques to create distinctive twentieth-century work.

Hamsun, Knut. *Growth of the Soil.* **New York: Knopf, 1921.**

Isak, a "lumbering barge of a man," looks for a homestead in northern Norway.

———. *Pan.* **New York: Knopf, 1921.**

With an introduction by Edward Bjorkman. Set in northern Norway, it has often been called Hamsun's most beautiful book.

Henrik Ibsen (1828–1906)

The founder of modern, realistic theater. Many of his plays deal with Norwegian domestic life.

Bryan, George B. *An Ibsen Companion: A Dictionary-Guide to the Life, Works, and Critical Reception of Henrik Ibsen.* **Westport, CT: Greenwood Press, 1984.**

Detailed entries on plays, films, characters, and figures in Ibsen's life. Includes a chronology and bibliography.

Fjelde, Rolf, ed. *Ibsen: The Complete Major Prose Plays.* **New York: Plume, 1978.**

Includes *Pillars of Society* (1877), *A Doll's House* (1879), *Ghosts* (1881), *An Enemy of the People* (1882), *The Wild Duck* (1884), *Rosmersholm* (1886), *The Lady from the Sea* (1888), *Hedda Gabler* (1890), *The Master Builder* (1892), *Little Eyolf* (1894), *John Gabriel Borkman* (1896), *When We Dead Awaken* (1899). Includes a bibliography and a stage history of Ibsen in the American theater.

Meyer, Michael. *Ibsen: A Biography.* **Garden City, NY: Doubleday, 1971.**

The definitive biography in English. Illustrations and bibliography.

Torborn Nedreaas (1906–)

One of the most important feminist writers in Norway.

Nedreaas, Torborn. *Nothing Grows by Moonlight*. Lincoln: University of Nebraska Press, 1987.

Called her "breakthrough novel," it deals with a young girl's struggle with a male-dominated society. Told in an unsentimental and ruggedly realistic manner.

Cora Sandel (1880–1974)

Lauded for her treatment of women characters, Sandel depicts their struggle for independence and the hostility of society. See the critical study by Ruth Essex, *Cora Sandel: Seeker of Truth*. New York: Peter Lang, 1995.

Sandel, Cora. *Alberta Alone*. New York: Orion Press, 1966.

Alberta struggles to rise above her narrow-minded middle-class milieu. Volume 3 of the Alberta trilogy.

———. *Alberta and Freedom*. London: Women's Press, 1980.

Volume 2 of the Alberta trilogy.

———. *Alberta and Jacob*. London: The Women's Press, 1980.

Volume 1 of the Alberta trilogy.

———. *Cora Sandel: Selected Short Stories*. Seattle: Seal Press, 1985.

A sampling of Sandel's short stories.

———. *The Leech*. Athens: Ohio University Press, 1986.

A continuation of the Alberta trilogy themes.

Sigrid Undset (1882–1949)

A Nobel Prize winner, Undset introduced the modern professional woman in her early realistic novels. She then produced two historical novels set in medieval Norway before returning to the contemporary world in several works about marriage and materialism.

Undset, Sigrid. *Kristin Lavransdatter: The Bridal Wreath, The Mistress of Husaby, The Cross.* **New York: Knopf, 1938.**

Includes explanatory notes and map. Set in the fourteenth century and focusing on Kristin Lavransdatter, with powerful poetic evocations of her youth, her marriage, and her political adventures.

————. *Return to the Future.* **New York: Knopf, 1942.**

A memoir covering Norway, spring 1940; Sweden, summer 1940; fourteen days in Russia; Japan en passant.

HISTORY OF SWEDEN

Andersen, Ingvar. *A History of Sweden.* **New York: Praeger, 1956.**

Chapters on early history, the Swedish Vikings, the coming of Christianity, the Middle Ages, the rule of Danish kings, problems of peace and war, relationship with Scandinavia, Charles XII, social problems and conflicts, Gustav III, Sweden during the Revolutionary Wars (1792–1809), the Romantic period, Scandinavianism, the beginnings of industrialism, Swedes abroad, the two World Wars.

Elder, Neil C. M. *Government in Sweden: The Executive at Work.* **New York: Pergamon Press, 1970.**

Chapters on the social democratic state, the role of the monarchy, the civil service, the legislative process, the courts, political style and political change. Bibliography.

Fleisher, Frederic. *The New Sweden: The Challenge of a Disciplined Democracy.* **New York: David McKay, 1967.**

See especially Chapter 1 for an overview of Sweden's history. Chapters on labor, business, social behavior, the arts and politics, the Swedish character. Bibliography.

Gustavson, Carl G. *The Small Giant: Sweden Enters the Industrial Era.* **Athens: Ohio University Press, 1986.**

The development of industrial Sweden from the early nineteenth century to 1914. Notes, bibliography, and register of persons.

Kennedy-Minott, Rodney. *Lonely Path to Follow: Nonaligned Sweden, United States/NATO, and the USSR.* **Stanford: Hoover Institution Press, 1990.**

A pamphlet on Sweden's attempts after World War II to steer a course between the Cold War adversaries, the United States and the Soviet Union.

Lewin, Leif. *Ideology and Strategy: A Century of Swedish Politics.* **Cambridge: Cambridge University Press, 1988.**

Chapters on suffrage, parliamentarism, economic planning, nuclear power, strategic actions in politics.

Moberg, Vilhelm. *A History of the Swedish People.* **New York: Pantheon Books, 1972.**

Chapters on the Swedish peasant, kings, seafarers, medieval people, and Scandinavia's greatest monarch (Margaret, Queen of the Union).

Roberts, Michael. *Essays in Swedish History.* **Minneapolis: University of Minnesota Press, 1967.**

Covers most historical periods up to the eighteenth century, and includes an essay on Swedish history in general.

Sather, Leland B., and Swanson, Alan. *Sweden.* **Santa Barbara, CA: Clio Press, 1987.**

Annotated bibliography on introductory works (older and recent descriptions, picture books, books for children);

geography (maps and atlases, glossaries, Sweden as part of Scandinavia, environment, tourism and travel); prehistory, archaeology and ethnography, history, population, religion, society, politics and government, foreign relations, economy, trade, industry, transport, agriculture and forestry, employment and labor, statistics, education, science and technology, languages, literature, the arts, music and dance, theater and film, sports and recreation, libraries, archives and museums, books and the media, periodicals and newspapers, encyclopedias. Map.

Scott, Franklin. *Sweden: The Nation's History*. Minneapolis: University of Minnesota Press, 1977.

Chapters on the beginnings of the land and the people, the Vikings, the coming of Christianity, medieval Sweden, the fifteenth and sixteenth centuries, Sweden's "Age of Greatness" (1611–1718), "The Age of Freedom" (1718–1771), the Gustavian Era (1746–1837), the Bernadotte Dynasty and the Union with Norway, the nineteenth century, World War I, the era of the welfare state, and the twentieth century. Bibliography and illustrations.

Tomasson, Richard F. *Sweden: Prototype of Modern Society*. New York: Random House, 1970.

Chapters on Swedish geography, population, and language; the state and politics; the religious situation; the schools; the universities and intellectual life; men, women, and the family; Swedish values.

TWENTIETH-CENTURY SWEDEN

Austin, Paul Britten. *On Being Swedish: Reflections towards a Better Understanding of the Swedish Character*. Coral Gables: University of Miami Press, 1968.

See introduction for comments on the Swedish personality. Chapters on society, nature, and a biographical dictionary of Swedes mentioned in the text.

Childs, Marquis. *Sweden: The Middle Way on Trial.* **New Haven: Yale University Press, 1980.**

See especially Chapter 1 for an evocative portrait of the Swedish land and people. Illustrations and bibliography.

Heclo, Hugh, and Madsen, Henrik. *Policy and Politics in Sweden: Principled Pragmatism.* **Philadelphia: Temple University Press, 1987.**

Chapters on Swedish innovation and rigidity, the Swedes' response to hard times, industrial relations, social welfare, housing policy, pragmatism, and purpose in social democracy. Bibliography.

Jenkins, David. *Sweden and the Price of Progress.* **New York: Coward-McCann, 1968.**

A study of Swedish socialism and welfare and the extent to which it serves as a model. Includes chapters on the Swedish woman and the artistic life.

SWEDISH BIOGRAPHY

Gustav Adolf (Gustavus Adolphus) *(1594–1632)*
This Swedish king, the second in the Vasa dynasty, fought wars in Denmark, Poland, and Russia and supported the Protestant cause in the Thirty Years' War. He established a national standing army and the Swedish navy.

Ahnlund, Nils. *Gustav Adolf the Great.* **Westport, CT: Greenwood Press, 1983. [First published in 1940.]**

A biography of one of the great Vasa kings, his rise to the throne, his marriage, the man and the monarch, his involvement in the Reformation, his contemporary reputation. Maps, illustrations, genealogical tree, bibliography.

Dupuy, Trevor Nevitt. *The Military Life of Gustavus Adolphus: Father of Modern War.* **New York: Franklin Watts, 1969.**

A detailed study of the military campaigns of one of the outstanding soldiers of world history. Chronology.

Charles XII (1682–1718)

Only fifteen years old when he became king, Charles XII won important battles against Poland and Russia and ruled briefly in Turkey.

Voltaire. *Lion of the North: Charles XII of Sweden*. East Brunswick, NJ: Associated University Presses, 1981.

> A translation of the great French writer's work, "an odd blend of respectful admiration and fascinated revulsion," as the translator M.F.O. Jenkins notes.

Queen Christina (1632–1654)

Christina ruled during a time of unrest in Sweden and Europe. She was known for her patronage of the arts.

Lewis, Paul. *Queen of Caprice: A Biography of Kristina of Sweden*. New York: Holt, Rinehart and Winston, 1962.

> A lively narrative of one of Sweden's most famous and controversial monarchs. Bibliography.

Mackenzie, Faith Compton. *The Sibyl of the North: The Tale of Christina, Queen of Sweden*. Boston: Houghton Mifflin, 1931.

> A biography narrated in gripping novel-like fashion. Illustrations and bibliography.

Masson, Georgina. *Queen Christina*. New York: Farrar, Straus & Giroux, 1968.

> One of the more detailed biographies of Sweden's famous monarch. Illustrations and bibliography.

Greta Garbo (1905–1990)

One of the most famous screen actresses, Garbo had a significant career in Sweden before coming to Hollywood.

Parris, Barry. *Garbo*. New York: Knopf, 1995.

> The most reliable and comprehensive biography yet published about the Swedish star.

Tyler, Parker. *Classics of the Foreign Film.* **New York: The Citadel Press, 1962.**

Contains a chapter about *The Story of Gosta Berling*, a silent film made from Selma Lagerlöf's novel, which stars Garbo.

Dag Hammarskjöld (1905–1961)

Secretary General of the United Nations (1953–1961). The son of a judge and former prime minister, Hammarskjöld had a distinguished career in banking and foreign affairs, participating in the Paris conference (1947) that established the Marshall Plan for the relief and rebuilding of Europe after World War II. He was actively involved in bringing peace to the Middle East (1957–1958) and was negotiating an end to the Congo crisis when his plane crashed in Zambia.

Beskow, Bo. *Dag Hammarskjöld: Strictly Personal, A Portrait.* **Garden City, NY: Doubleday, 1969.**

Illustrations.

Simon, Charlie May. *Dag Hammarskjöld.* **New York: Dutton, 1967.**

Illustrations and bibliography.

Soderberg, Sten. *Hammarskjöld: A Pictorial Biography.* **New York: Viking, 1962.**

Illustrations.

Van Dusen, Henry P. *Dag Hammarskjöld: The Statesman and His Faith.* **New York: Harper & Row, 1967.**

Illustrations.

Alfred Nobel (1833–1896)

Chemist and inventor, Nobel distinguished himself in the development of explosives. Later, he had misgivings about his participation in the creation of instruments of war. On his death he left a fund establishing annual awards for important work in physics, chemistry, physiology and medicine, literature, and the promotion of international peace.

Bergengren, Erik. *Alfred Nobel: The Man and His Work.* **New York: T. Nelson, 1962.**

Illustrations and bibliography. Includes an essay on the Nobel prizes.

Fant, Kenne. *Alfred Nobel: A Biography.* **New York: Arcade, 1993.**

Illustrations.

Halas, Nicholas. *Nobel: A Biography.* **London: R. Hale, 1959.**

Illustrations.

Raoul Wallenberg (1912–?)

Honored for his efforts to save the lives of Hungarian Jews, this businessman and diplomat disappeared while in Russian custody. His death has not been verified.

Anger, Per. *With Raoul Wallenberg in Budapest: Memories of the War Years in Hungary.* **New York: Holocaust Library, 1981.**

Author Per Anger collaborated with Wallenberg in rescuing Hungarian Jews from Nazi death camps. He describes what happened and what should have been done from the Swedish side to rescue Wallenberg, who was incarcerated by the Russians and vanished.

Bierman, John. *Righteous Gentile: The Story of Raoul Wallenberg, Missing Hero of the Holocaust.* **New York: Viking, 1981.**

Begins with a description of the Holocaust and then describes the role Wallenberg played trying to save Hungarian Jews. Written with the cooperation of Wallenberg's half-sister, government officials, and Holocaust historians.

Marton, Kati. *Wallenberg.* **New York: Random House, 1982.**

Based on extensive travel and interviews in Budapest, Vienna, Munich, Brussels, London, and New York. Includes chapters on his youth and early career. Chapter notes and bibliography.

Wallenberg, Raoul. *Letters and Dispatches 1924–1944.* **New York: Arcade Publishing, 1995.**

Wallenberg's written record of his efforts to save Jews from extermination.

SWEDISH LITERATURE

Bly, Robert, ed. *Friends, You Drank Some Darkness: Three Swedish Poets, Harry Martinson, Gunnar Ekelof, and Tomas Transtromer.* **Boston: Beacon Press, 1975.**

Bly, a prolific editor and collector of poetry, has here focused his efforts on the work of three Swedes.

Gustafson, Alrik. *History of Swedish Literature.* **Minneapolis: University of Minnesota Press, 1961.**

From the origins of Swedish literature to modernism, with chapters on the Middle Ages, religious reformation and cultural decline, political expansion and literary renaissance, the Enlightenment, romanticism, Strindberg, realism. A list of translations in English, a pronunciation guide, illustrations, and bibliography.

Karin Boye (1900–1941)
Her writing exhibits a religious intensity and explores the ways to salvation.

Boye, Karin. *Kallocain.* **Madison: University of Wisconsin Press, 1966.**

A utopian novel based on Boye's travels in Germany and the Soviet Union that has been compared to Aldous

Huxley's *Brave New World* (1932) and to Franz Kafka's novels.

Stig Dagerman (1923–1954)

One of the most important postwar writers whose themes show the extremity of coping with the war's aftermath.

Dagerman, Stig. *A Burnt Child*. New York: Morrow, 1950.

The story of a motherless youth told with probing psychological perception.

———. *The Games of Night: Ten Stories and an Autobiographical Piece*. Philadelphia: Lippincott, 1961.

Permeated with fear and an atmosphere of death.

Rolf Edberg (1912–)

An environmental writer.

Edberg, Rolf. *On the Shred of a Cloud*. University, AL: University of Alabama Press, 1969.

A plea for environmental preservation studded with evocative descriptions of the Scandinavian landscape.

Vilhelm Eklund (1880–1949)

A nature poet, influenced by French symbolist poets and the German philosopher Nietzsche.

Eklund, Vilhelm. *The Second Light*. San Francisco: North Point Press, 1986.

Per Olov Enquist (1934–)

A self-reflexive writer who has taken on many different subjects, but who is interested in the nature of narrative and how it both reveals and conceals the writer.

Enquist, Per Olov. *The Legionnaires: A Documentary Novel*. New York: Delacorte, 1973.

The author's international success, set in 1946, examining

the Swedish government's return of Baltic prisoners to the Soviet Union.

————. *The Night of the Tribades*. **New York: Dramatists Play Service, 1978.**

About the struggle of August Strindberg and his wife, Siri von Essen, during a rehearsal of a play about their lives.

Pär Lagerkvist (1891–1974)

A Nobel Prize winner, translated into at least thirty-four languages. Playwright, poet, and novelist, a great modernist and philosophical writer noted for his religious and existential themes.

Lagerkvist, Pär. *Barabbas*. **New York: Random House, 1951.**

A novel about the robber who was set free when Jesus was crucified. Explores Barabbas's spiritual crisis.

————. *The Death of Ahasuerus*. **New York: Random House, 1962.**

One of the novelist's series of religious novels about the search for peace. See also *Pilgrim at Sea*, *The Holy Land*, and *Mariamne*.

Selma Lagerlöf (1858–1940)

This Nobel Prize winner is known best for her fiction set in Varmland, a west-central Swedish province. An optimistic writer of considerable narrative drive with an interest in folklore. See the introductory study by Vivi Edstrom, *Selma Lagerlöf*. Boston: Twayne, 1984. Includes a biographical chapter, chronology, notes, and bibliography. See also the entries in Scandinavian literature and Hanna Larsen, *Selma Lagerlöf*. Garden City, NY: Doubleday Doran, 1936. Includes a chronological checklist of the books of Selma Lagerlöf published in the United States.

Lagerlöf, Selma. *Diary of Selma Lagerlöf.* New York: Doubleday Doran, 1936.

Continuation of *Mårbacka.* (See below.)

————. *From a Swedish Homestead.* New York: McClure, 1901.

The story of a country house called Queens on the site of the great Kungahalla, featuring the forest queen Sigrid Storrada.

————. *The Girl from the March.* Garden City, NY: Doubleday Page, 1916.

Short stories based on legends and tales of the countryside.

————. *Mårbacka.* Garden City, NY: Doubleday Doran, 1924.

A volume of Lagerlöf's autobiography dealing with her parents, brothers and sisters, family servants, and with the originals of some of the characters in her fiction.

————. *Memories of My Childhood: Further Years at Mårbacka.* Garden City, NY: Doubleday Doran, 1934.

————. *The Ring of the Löwenskölds.* [Trilogy.] *The General's Ring, Charlotte Löwensköld, Anna Svård.* Garden City, NY: Doubleday Doran, 1931.

Set in Varmland, a humorous story of the Swedish countryside, with strong female characters, and an exploration of religious themes.

————. *The Story of Gösta Berling.* Stockholm: Fritzes Kungl, 1959.

A modern lyrical and dramatic epic. Pastor Berling is the ambiguous, often morally impugned hero of loosely linked tales set in Varmland.

————. *The Wonderful Adventures of Nils.* New York: Doubleday Page, 1907.

Illustrations. Written as a geography for elementary school children, featuring Nils, a rude farm boy who is turned into Tom Thumb and carried off by a wild goose. Contains superb descriptions of the cities and the countryside.

Sara Lidman (1923–   )

Her work has been called an example of "neo-provincialism." Set in her native Vasterbotten, her novels deal with human outcasts.

Lidman, Sara. *The Rain Bird*. New York: G. Braziller, 1962.

The main character is a musician, Linda Stahl, facing the dilemmas of homosexual love. Praised as a high point in the Swedish psychological novel.

Vilhelm Moberg (1898–1973)

Celebrated for his novels of the rural Swedish peasantry (farmers, soldiers, and emigrants). The son of a crofting family, he bases his vivid descriptions of this life on firsthand experience and on his heritage. See the introductory study by Philip Holmes, *Vilhelm Moberg*. Boston: Twayne, 1980. Includes a biographical chapter, studies of his most important work, a chronology, notes, and bibliography.

Moberg, Vilhelm. *The Emigrants*. New York: Simon & Schuster, 1951.

Filmed by Jan Troell in 1972–1973, this novel is about nineteenth-century Swedish farmers in the United States.

———. *Unto a Good Land*. New York: Simon & Schuster, 1954.

A continuation of *The Emigrants*.

———. *When I Was a Child*. New York: Knopf, 1956.

Documents the history of the labor movement, in which Moberg took part.

A Scandinavian American Photo Album

"Scandinavia" is the term used to describe five countries—Denmark, Finland, Iceland, Norway, and Sweden—with distinct yet intertwined cultures and histories. Harsh but beautiful winters, geographic isolation, and forbidding landscapes forged a hardy, adaptable, and innovative people. These qualities facilitated the relatively smooth assimilation of Scandinavian immigrants into the United States. Many became farmers in midwestern states in the second half of the nineteenth century. But becoming American did not mean a loss of Scandinavian identity. Scandinavian Americans are rightfully proud of their heritage and traditions, which they have shared with the rest of the world. The Nordic region's rich storytelling tradition produced folktales, myths, sagas, and epics popular with children and adults everywhere. One can easily see the region's expansive natural beauty reflected in Scandinavian design, architecture, art, and music. Perhaps your interest in your Scandinavian heritage will inspire you to plan a visit to the land of your ancestors. But you need not travel that far—celebrations of Scandinavia are enjoyed by Scandinavian Americans around the country, throughout the year.

The Vikings, a Scandinavian warrior people, were famed raiders and explorers. They reputedly landed in the area now known as New England between the ninth and eleventh centuries. During this period, now known as the Viking Age, the Vikings were the finest shipbuilders and sailors in the world. Above, Edward Moran's painting depicts Viking longships. Each longship was usually adorned with the figure of an animal on its high prow and round shields on its sides. Longships could travel great distances, with their wide sails and crews of up to thirty oarsmen.

In Frederikssund, Denmark, Danes celebrate their Viking heritage with an annual seventeen-day Viking Festival that begins in late June and runs through the beginning of July. During the festival, up to 200 local participants re-create a Viking village, dress in traditional attire, and stage theater demonstrations of Viking fighting, stories, and daily life for spectators from around the world. A Danish theater troupe also tours the globe performing its Viking spectacle.

Scandinavians tradtionally celebrate the summer solstice, the longest day of the year. It is widely referred to as midsummer. The festivities, which include bonfires, dancing, singing, boat rides, lakeside activities, and food and drink, often go on all night.

Helsinki, the capital of Finland, is also Finland's commercial and intellectual center, boasting a number of industrial plants and a major university. Pictured above is Helsinki's impressive railway station, designed by the renowned Finnish American architect Eliel Saarinen in 1914.

Scandinavian countries stand out for the number of women who hold important positions in government. Elisabeth Rehn, a member of the Finnish Parliament since 1979, held the post of Minister of Defense of Finland from 1990 to 1991. Other Scandinavian women leaders include the prime minister of Norway, Gro Harlem Brundtland, and the president of Iceland, Vigdis Finnbogadottir.

Sweden's capital, Stockholm, is the country's largest city and also its economic, administrative, and cultural center. Stockholm is often called the "Venice of the North" because, like Venice, it is built on several peninsulas and islands, and has many bridges and boats for crossing the water. The Nobel prizes (except the Nobel Peace Prize) are awarded in Stockholm every year.

The province of Skåne, in southern Sweden, was the sight of many battles between Denmark and Sweden until it was conquered by Charles X of Sweden in 1658. An important historic sight in Skåne is the Ales Stenar, above. It is the largest Scandinavian tumulus, or burial mound, in which a ship was buried along with its captain. It is ringed by giant stone slabs, probably dating from the Bronze Age.

Norway is famous for its breathtaking fjords, narrow inlets of sea between cliffs. The 110-mile-long and 4,000-foot-deep Sogne Fjord is the longest and deepest in Norway. The beauty of this region, with its sheer mountain walls dropping to the surface of the water, makes the Sogne Fjord a popular tourist site. Many famous resorts are perched along its banks.

In Scandinavian folklore, trolls were friendly or malicious creatures who were said to live in caves and hills. In Norway, the troll has become a national symbol and is often represented by a statuette, like the one above.

Iceland is a country rich in natural wonders such as geysers, volcanoes, hot springs, and glaciers. Above, a team of explorers emerges from a volcanic ice cave in the Kaldaklofs-Jokull glacier in south-central Iceland. These enormous caves of ice were formed by a stream of molten lava.

Traditional Icelandic sod houses have walls and roofs consisting of stacked strips of sod. The strong roots of the sod hold the houses together remarkably well (except in heavy rains, whereafter they usually have to be replaced), and provide excellent protection against fire, wind, heat, and cold. These sod houses are part of an exhibit at the Skogar Folk Museum in Skogar, Iceland.

The Saami, once known as Laplanders, are a pastoral people who live in the northern reaches of Norway, Sweden, and Finland. They are indigenous to the Scandinavian region. Many Saami still maintain a traditional lifestyle, dressing as their ancestors did, living in tents, and herding reindeer.

Located on the California central coast, the village of Solvang was founded by Danish immigrants in 1900. Every year, on the third weekend of September, Solvang celebrates its Danish heritage with a festival called Danish Days. People from around the globe gather to participate in traditional dances, tell stories, and feast on Danish foods.

Finnish American actress Christine Lahti appeared on Broadway in Wendy Wasserstein's Tony Award and Pulitzer Prize-winning play *The Heidi Chronicles*. She has also appeared in many films, including *Running on Empty* and *The Doctor*, and has received acclaim for her work on the television show *Chicago Hope*. In 1984, Lahti was nominated for an Oscar for Best Supporting Actress in *Swing Shift* for her portrayal of a housewife who becomes a factory worker during World War II.

A native of Anoka, Minnesota, author and radio personality Garrison Keillor brought his home
state and its large Scandinavian American community into the American popular consciousness
with his widely broadcast radio program, *Prairie Home Companion,* and his series of novels,
including *Lake Wobegon Days.*

Sigfrid Siwertz (1882–1970)

His fiction is set in Stockholm and evokes an exquisite sense of the historical period.

Siwertz, Sigfrid. *Downstream*. New York: Knopf, 1923.

A Freudian study of five siblings.

August Strindberg (1849–1912)

One of the giants of modern theater, Strindberg was also a novelist and essayist. Often accused of misogyny, he probes deeply into the problems of family life and the relationships between men and women, husbands and wives.

Johannesson, Eric O. *The Novels of August Strindberg: A Study in Theme and Structure*. Berkeley: University of California Press, 1968.

Concentrates on the theme of the quest for destiny and the autobiographical elements in the fiction. Chapters on *The Red Room, Progress, The Son of a Servant, The People of Memso, The Defense of a Fool, The Romantic Organist, Tschandala, A Witch, By the Open Sea, Inferno, Alone, Black Banners, The Roofing Feast, The Scapegoat*. Bibliography and index of proper names.

Johnson, Walter. *August Strindberg*, Boston: Twayne, 1976.

Includes a biographical chapter, studies of his major works, a chronology, notes, and bibliography.

Lagercrantz, Olof. *August Strindberg*. New York: Farrar Straus & Giroux, 1984.

A succinct biography, copiously illustrated. Notes and bibliography.

Meyer, Michael. *Strindberg*. New York: Random House, 1985.

A comprehensive, scholarly biography, with illustrations, notes, and bibliography.

Sprinchorn, Evert, ed. *August Strindberg: Selected Plays*. **Minneapolis: University of Minnesota Press, 1986.**

> *Master Olof, The Father, Miss Julie, Creditors, The Stronger, Playing with Fire, To Damascus, Crimes and Crimes, The Dance of Death, A Dream Play, The Ghost Sonata, The Pelican.* Introductions to each play and a bibliography.

Chapter 3
Beginning Your Genealogical Search

Clarify the most basic facts about your family before you begin—even your family name. The business of unraveling names is especially difficult in Scandinavia. The situation is complicated by changing sovereigns: Finland, for example, was a province of Sweden (Swedish is still one of the official languages of Finland) until 1809, when it was taken over by the Russians, who did not cede back all the territory they had annexed until 1956. To make matters more complicated, all Scandinavian countries originally adhered to the custom of patronymics; that is, adopting a modified form of the father's given name as a surname. In Denmark and Norway, for example, Clara, daughter of Jens, was called Clara Jensdatter, and Andreas, son of Svein, was called Andreas Sveinssen. (Swedes added "-dotter" and "-son" for the same purposes.) Given the small number of common Scandinavian given names, the result was often tens of thousands of Clara Jensdatters. The patronymics system was ended by legislation in Sweden and Norway in the early twentieth century.

To counteract the confusion, governments of Scandinavian countries adopted various naming policies. In 1856, Denmark decreed that all patronymics would end in "-sen." By that time, however, the patronymic system had already begun to disappear, as many Danes—particularly those in the southern part of the country—adopted the German custom of using an established surname. Still, Danish records dating from the middle of the eighteenth to the middle of the nineteenth century often list established surnames as well as patronymics, plus other identifying monikers, such as "the old" or "the young."

Although Danes were known to employ the names of their professions or home parishes as part of their designations, this system was elaborated in Norway, where individuals often added the name of their farm (either the one where they were born or one occupied most recently), an occupational name (e.g., "Smed" for "Smith"), and even a "student" name (a Latinized version of their patronymic; e.g., "Danielius" for "Danielssen").

If you are of Icelandic ancestry, be advised that the use of patronymics persists in that country, which officially grants its citizens the use of one or two Icelandic names. The Reykjavik telephone book would list Tryggvi Thoroddsen, for example, under both "T" and "Th."

It is useful to bear in mind a few other Scandinavian naming nuances when researching early records: Women were customarily listed under their maiden name (that is, using a patronymic derived from their father's given name); children do not always use the same farm name as their father; and Scandinavian names can include letters modified with diacritical marks (such as an å) that can be transliterated in various ways. As was the case with many other immigrant groups, Scandinavians often changed their names after arriving in the United States, so that Esbjorn Hakanson might become Osborn Hawkinson. Several of the books listed in the **Resources** section below contain lists of Scandinavian names—including those that are foreign-influenced—with Americanized equivalents.

The First Sketch

Now start with yourself. Take a sheet of $8\frac{1}{2} \times 11$-inch looseleaf paper. Write down your full name and date and place of birth. You can, of course, use a word processing program to record information. Be sure, however, to keep a hard (paper) copy set of files not only as backup (in case your computer files are destroyed), but as a sample to show your family and other genealogical researchers. You might also want to write a genealogical sketch, putting down what you have been told about your family history. List the *sources* of your information: parents, other relatives, neighbors, family friends. Be as specific as possible: cite your sources by their full names, explaining their relationship to you, where they live (or lived), and anything else that might identify them. For example, if you have an older brother who tells you something about another relative, or about himself, be sure to identify him as your *source* and explain how he came by his information.

Here is an example of a first try at a genealogical/family history sketch. Carl Rollyson has tried to reconstruct what he has been told about his family history and Scandinavian heritage (from his father's side of the family). Notice that much of his information, to begin with, is vague. He is relying on memory and on information that may turn out to be inaccurate. But he is recording as much potential data as possible and identifying areas of research. This initial sketch will also function as a measuring point that shows how he began his genealogical/family history search.

> My Aunt Iva, my father's oldest sister, was the family historian. She lived most of her life in Morgan, West Virginia. She was a teacher, and her husband, Edward Tomlinson, was an insurance agent for New York Life. She mentioned that the Rollyson name had a Norwegian origin; it stemmed, she believed, from the Norwegian conqueror Rollo. But most of her information about the Rollysons stemmed from the Civil War period. She told me that her grandmother was a Chapman (Irish) and married a Rollyson (his ancestry is not clear from her brief, written family history). I know from reading histories of West Virginia that many of the settlers were Scotch-Irish. If I can find where the first Rollysons settled in the United States, I can begin to find out at what point my Scandinavian ancestors mingled with other ethnic groups. My Aunt Iva's guess was that Rollyson was an English form of a Scandinavian name.

That is only the beginning of a genealogical/family history sketch. You may find, as Carl did, that the act of writing it

As you complete a family history sketch, try to think about how your family was affected by historical events involving Scandinavia and Scandinavian Americans. Here, Finnish Americans organize donations of goods to be sent to Finland during its war with the Soviet Union in 1939–40.

down begins to call forth many more details than you thought were in your grasp. For example, as he was writing the sketch, Carl remembered that on a trip to visit his Aunt Iva he saw a sign for Rollyson, West Virginia, "Population 3." He was fourteen years old at the time and was intrigued by finding his name on such a sign; now that recollected detail may become part of the vital link in retracing his roots. Although several of his family members have died, including his Aunt Iva, he has place names in her written record and others she mentioned to him that he can check on maps or perhaps even visit. His uncle, Edward Tomlinson, was a prominent citizen and a successful busi-nessman, and Carl might be able to interview people who knew his uncle and who may recall a few facts about the Rollysons or about the period in West Virginia history when Carl's family first settled there.

One other result of beginning with a genealogical sketch is

that you may realize that you are dealing with more than one ethnic group. Indeed, Carl may learn a great deal more about his Scotch-Irish background than he does about his Norwegian origins. On the other hand, what Carl will find should not be prejudged.

Like any genealogical investigator, begin by listing as many names, places, and dates or historical periods (i.e., Civil War period, before World War I, etc.) as you can. Gradually the initial, vague, genealogical/family history sketch will become a manageable project. Think of the genealogical search as a research paper with a theme. What is your theme? How much of it can you explore in one project? Which side of the family interests you more, or which side is likely to yield the most data? But you don't have to answer all of these questions at once. Simply writing out the preliminary genealogical sketch will help you to decide, and revisions of that sketch will help you to decide on the focus of your project.

It is easy to forget genealogical details and family history anecdotes; writing them down makes a record that will come in handy when you interview your sources and learn things from other family members. Treat yourself as a *subject*. Create a *subject* file not only for yourself, but for other members of your family and for your descendants.

Creating Files

Make subject files of information about your brothers and sisters and parents. Put in each file looseleaf papers or printouts and photocopies of documents such as birth and baptismal certificates, employment records, school report cards, award certificates, newspaper clippings with birth announcements and obituaries, announcements of engagements and marriages, old letters, diaries, address books, photographs, passports, burial records, military discharge papers, and other pieces of information. These scattered records will eventually tell the story of your family.

Check first with family members to see what records they may have. Most people have their birth certificates, and

Military records are an important addition to an individual's file. These Norwegian Americans volunteered to go to the front lines if fighting spread to Norway in World War II.

sometimes the birth certificates of their parents if their parents have died. Similarly, you may find that family members have death certificates, since such documents are often needed for insurance purposes and legal matters. Many families rent safe-deposit boxes for important papers.

Be sure to standardize your records. Write or photocopy all information on the same size paper so that it can eventually be put into a looseleaf binder with dividers. It is preferable to photocopy any document a family member gives you, in case the original is misplaced. If photocopying is expensive or inconvenient, take extreme care in filing and storing originals.

Tracking Down Information

Your local librarian can help you locate the sources of other records—such as military discharge papers, employment records, and burial records. Libraries may also direct you to books (such as the ones listed in the **Resources** section) that give specific addresses or explain how to contact agencies with the information you need. Compile as much detailed information as possible before you begin a

library search. Make sure you know which branch of the military a relative served in, or where he or she was employed, what company he or she worked for, and so on.
At larger libraries, you will also find telephone books for major cities. Under the pages for state and local government you will find listings for vital records units—those departments that issue birth or death certificates. Other agencies, such as a department of motor vehicles, may also have information that is accessible to the public. Such records may yield important facts about where family members lived and worked. Think of the telephone book as an important resource; it may save you countless trips to the wrong places, and just by talking to people in various offices you will begin to get a sense of how governments and communities arrange their records. Often, vital records will be held at the courthouse in the county where the event took place.

How Far Back to Go?

Scandinavian Americans usually have a parent, grandparent, or great-grandparent who immigrated to the United States. It will be quite a task to document three or four generations—yours, your parents', your grandparents', and your great-grandparents'. You may choose to work back from the present to the point at which your ancestor emigrated from Scandinavia to the United States. You may also become interested in the history of your family in Scandinavia beyond your grandparents' or great-grandparents' generation. Genealogical research in Scandinavia, however, may involve considerable correspondence and perhaps even travel to Denmark, Finland, Iceland, Norway, or Sweden.

Before you do so, however, there are a number of resources to be tapped here in the United States. For information on individual countries, you can contact the following:

Danish Consulate General
885 Second Avenue, 18th Floor
New York, NY 10017
212-223-4545

Finnish Consulate General
866 United Nations Plaza, Suite 250
New York, NY 10017
212-750-4400

Icelandic Consulate General
800 Third Avenue, 36th Floor
New York, NY 10022
212-593-2700

Norwegian Information Service
825 Third Avenue, 38th Floor
New York, NY 10017
212-421-7333

Swedish Information Service
885 Second Avenue
New York, NY 10017
212-751-5900

These consulates and information services can provide you with information about travel in Scandinavia, church records, and the addresses of public archives and records units to which you can write for genealogical information. There is also an American Scandinavian Foundation that can provide information about cultural exchanges. The Foundation no longer sponsors the publication of books on Scandinavia (many of which are listed in the **Resources** sections), but it still should be contacted if you are interested in specific aspects of Scandinavian history or in particular historical figures. It is located at 725 Park Avenue, 7th Floor, New York, NY 10021, telephone number, 212-879-9779.

Time and money may affect the depth of your search. You can expect to pay fees for photocopies of documents. Fees may be charged for genealogical searches in Scandinavian countries. In this country, a copy of a single record may cost $5 or $10. So it is important to see what records your family already has. You might also want to make up a budget for your genealogical search. How much are you willing to spend on records, on long-distance phone calls, and on travel?

There may be a wealth of genealogical information right in your own home. A family Bible may contain names, dates of birth, or other significant events in your family's history. Scrapbooks, high school yearbooks, and photographs can provide clues to events, names, and dates. An old trunk could contain letters long forgotten. Even a postcard with a date stamp on it can lead to verifying key events in your family history or the whereabouts of relatives. Souvenirs and trinkets, while not necessarily providing factual information, can be revealing of the family's character.

Setting a Goal and Moving Ahead

When you have gathered all the vital records and documents that you can, think about your goal for your project. Are you interested in simply tracing your roots and finding out who you are related to, how many cousins you have, what parts of the country your family settled in, and so on? Or do you wish to write a family history, detailing some of the significant experiences of two, three, or four generations of Scandinavian Americans? Writing a family history is a much more ambitious project than creating a genealogy.

Another option is to photocopy parts of the family Bible or family photographs and make a family tree out of them. Letters could also be photocopied and quoted from.

By proceeding step by step, beginning with yourself and working backward, you can maintain flexibility. Work first as a genealogist and then see how much of a family historian you want to become. There may be members of the family who are willing to help you write your family history. Think about what kind of project would be most enjoyable for you, and speak to your strengths and interests.

Clubs, churches, labor unions, or other organizations to which your relatives may have belonged may have records of their activities. See if the organization has an archive of newsletters, newspaper clippings, or minutes from meetings,

The Norwegian Lutheran Church in Telemark, New Jersey, was typical of many churches that served as focal points for immigrant communities. Church records can be valuable sources of information on birth, death, marriage, and baptism dates.

for example. You may be able to learn more about relatives' interests and hobbies in this way.

Library Research

After gathering all the information you can from your home and community sources, such as courthouses, your next step will be library and public archive research. First, try your local library; it will have certain basic books about genealogical research and family history. It may even have a separate genealogy or local history department. Your city may have a regional branch of the Family History Library operated by The Church of Jesus Christ of Latter-day Saints (LDS), also known as the Mormons, located in Salt Lake City, Utah. These Family History Centers have access to the main library's vast genealogical holdings. At a Family History Center you can also sign up on a Family Registry, a request for information about a certain family line.

Don't be discouraged if your local library offers little specific information about your family. If possible, go to the library's main branch in your city or county. Larger libraries may have more genealogical materials or librarians who are knowledgeable about genealogical searches. The computer catalog of a library's holdings may allow you to search for materials outside of your library system, which the librarian may help you to obtain through interlibrary loan.

The National Archives in Washington, DC, or one of its regional branches contain many useful records for genealogists, such as census records. Although it can be a challenge to locate a relative's name in the census, you will be rewarded with a listing of full names of household members, birthplaces, years of residence in the United States, occupation, and other important details. You may be able to order photocopies of certain census pages from the National Archives. In addition, a large research library may have copies of censuses.

The **Resources** listed at the end of this chapter will guide you to the sources of mortgage papers, tax records, lawsuits, deeds, and other records that will help you piece together your family's life in the United States. You will probably find that the research process goes more smoothly as you progress. You'll gradually become more comfortable with using libraries, archives, books, and other genealogical sources. Never be afraid to ask questions; your fellow genealogists, in particular, will probably be happy to give you advice. Speak up when you need help from librarians, too. Their job is to make sure that you get the most from the library's resources, and they will be eager to guide you.

Resources

GENEALOGICAL TOOLS

Several general reference works and journals will be helpful in your genealogical search. Only large public or research libraries are likely to have many of these publications. But ask your local or school librarian about obtaining the following items through interlibrary loan:

Allen, Desmond Walls, and Billingsley, Carolyn Earle. *Beginner's Guide to Family History Research.* **Bountiful, UT: American Genealogical Lending Library, 1991.**

> A comprehensive introduction to genealogy. Chapters cover home and family sources, organizing family records, using libraries and archives, census records, courthouse research, military records, ethnic genealogy, how to manage correspondence and queries, adoptee searches for natural parents. Includes samples of how to record family data, a glossary, and a bibliography.

American Genealogical Lending Library
P.O. Box 244
Bountiful, UT 84010

> The library is part of an effort by the Mormons (the Church of Jesus Christ of Latter-day Saints) to compile repositories of genealogical records around the country. Check your local telephone directory or ask your local librarian to find out if the LDS Church has a Family History Center near you. The library in Bountiful rents census microfilm and has other rental programs that help with genealogical research. It has also developed a computer program, Personal Ancestry File, to manage genealogical research.

Baxter, Angus. *In Search of Your European Roots: A Complete Guide to Tracing Your Ancestors in Every Country in Europe.* **Baltimore: Genealogical Publishing Co., 1986.**

See especially chapters on Finland (pp. 75–80) and Iceland (pp. 161–164). Brief chapters on Denmark, Norway, and Sweden, but this book is one of the only readily available, up-to-date sources in English that address Finnish and Icelandic genealogy. Includes brief historical overview, annotated lists of resources (with addresses), and helpful hints on the peculiarities of researching genealogy in these countries.

Carlberg, Nancy Ellen. *Beginning Norwegian Research.* **Anaheim, CA: Carlberg Press, 1991.**

A comprehensive guide, including a list of common male and female names, list of counties and regions (together with maps of old and new Norwegian counties), a calendar of feast days, guides to setting up a filing system, sample record forms, sample forms for photoduplication orders at the Mormon Family History Library, chapters on searching U.S. and Norwegian sources, sample records (such as a marriage license, census schedule, and parish register), sample pedigree chart and family group sheet.

———. *Overcoming Dead Ends.* **Anaheim, CA: Carlberg Press, 1991.**

Helpful information about what to do when your research seems to have ended. Describes how to analyze a family group sheet, what types of records to pursue and what clues to look for.

———. *Researching in Salt Lake City.* **Anaheim, CA: Carlberg Press, 1987.**

(Updated yearly.) Tips on how to use the Family History Library in Salt Lake City, Utah. Includes information on how to prepare for a visit, how to get there, library rules, and how to use the library in person or through the mail.

Choquette, Margarita, et al. *The Beginner's Guide to Finnish Genealogical Research*. Bountiful, UT: Thomsen's Genealogical Center, 1985.

> Provides lists of resources, such as church and emigration records, together with addresses of archives, libraries, genealogical societies, and researchers. Especially helpful are translations of Finnish genealogical terms into English.

Dine, L. G. *The Genealogist's Encyclopedia*. New York: Weybright and Talley, 1969.

> Chapters on genealogy and the oral tradition, records in several European countries, heraldry, titles, a glossary of key terms, and illustrations.

Directory of Archives and Manuscript Repositories in the United States. Washington, DC: National Archives and Records Service, 1978.

> Organized by state. A valuable list of addresses and phone numbers for libraries, historical societies, museums, and other repositories of manuscripts. A typical entry will describe the repository's major holdings, its size, and cite other repositories that house similar material. Hours, terms of access (in some cases, special permission is required), and the availability of copying services are also noted.

Doane, Gilbert. *Searching for Your Ancestors: The How and Why of Genealogy*. Minneapolis: University of Minnesota Press, 1960.

> Chapters on family papers, town records, inscriptions in cemeteries, church records, government aid in research, how to arrange a genealogy. Appendixes on bibliographies, locations of vital statistics, census records, records dating back to the Revolutionary War.

Dollarhide, William. *Managing a Genealogical Project*. Baltimore: Genealogical Publishing Co., 1988.

Contains a list of sample forms (relationship chart, family data sheet, research log, ancestor table, research journal, correspondence log), types of genealogical projects and a glossary of genealogical relationships, collecting references (basic rules in note-taking), evaluating genealogical evidence, using a computer, presentation techniques (pedigrees, biographies).

Family History Centers. For a list of locations, send a stamped, self-addressed envelope to:
Family History Library
35 North West Temple Street
Salt Lake City, UT 84150

Gateway to America: Genealogical Research in the New York State Library. **Albany: New York State Library, 1980.**

Contains a section on genealogical research in the state library, a helpful introduction to searching and recording genealogical information or "forms for record," a helpful explanation of how genealogical works and records are organized, a listing of important books with their call numbers, floor diagrams of the library, a list of leading genealogical periodicals, and guides to local and state records.

Greenwood, Val D. *The Researcher's Guide to American Genealogy.* **Baltimore: Genealogical Publishing Co., 1973.**

Several chapters on methods of research, different kinds of records, using libraries and archives, interpreting data, writing letters of inquiry about genealogical research, how to organize a "research calendar." Many samples of records are shown and explained.

Hanks, Patricia, and Hodges, Flavia. *A Dictionary of First Names.* **New York: Oxford University Press, 1990.**

An extensive survey of more than 4,500 European and American names, giving the linguistic and ethnic root and usually the non-English form of the name. Diminutive (shortened) and pet names are also included.

————. *A Dictionary of Surnames*. New York: Oxford University Press, 1989.

An important source for genealogists and family historians, especially for those searching for relatives whose names may have more than one national origin (e.g., Finns living in the "Lost Territories"). A survey of the origins of 100,000 surnames of European origin as they are currently found throughout the world.

Hey, David. *The Oxford Guide to Family History*. New York: Oxford University Press, 1993.

A guide to constructing a family tree, with an account of how families have functioned in history, chapters on researching court and municipal records and church registers, and the origins of family names.

Hjelm, Dennis J. *Especially for Swedes*. Author, 1985.

In addition to guidance on how to begin your Swedish genealogical research, this book devotes separate chapters to the major avenues of inquiry: parish, birth, marriage, death, probate, court, land, census, tax, and military records. Introductory sections provide helpful information on nuances of the Swedish language, how to read Gothic script, patronymics, military names, farm, place, and trade names, given names, and surname changes in the United States.

Kemp, Thomas J. *Vital Records Handbook*. Baltimore: Genealogical Publishing Co., 1988.

Addresses and phone numbers for vital records; the cost of obtaining records such as birth, death, and marriage certificates; copies of state forms requesting vital statistics. Arranged alphabetically by state. Separate section on Canadian provinces.

National Archives and Records Administration
Washington, DC 20408

Request several free leaflets: *Military Services Records in the National Archives, Using Records in the National Archives for Genealogical Research,* and *Getting Started: Beginning Your Genealogical Research in the National Archives in Washington.* The National Archives store censuses, vital records, and other documents useful to genealogists.

National Archives Regional Archives
Central Plains
2312 East Bannister Road
Kansas City, MO 64131
816-926-6272

Contains information on Iowa, Kansas, Missouri, Nebraska.

Great Lakes
7358 South Pulaski Road
Chicago, IL 60629
312-581-7816

Contains information on Illinois, Indiana, Michigan, Minnesota, Ohio, Wisconsin.

Mid-Atlantic
Ninth and Market Streets
Philadelphia, PA 19107
215-597-3000

Contains information on Delaware, Maryland, Pennsylvania, Virginia, West Virginia.

New England
380 Trapelo Road
Waltham, MA 02154
617-647-8100

Contains information on Connecticut, Maine, Massachusetts, New Hampshire, Rhode Island, Vermont.

Northeast
Building 22—MOT Bayonne
Bayonne, NJ 07002-5388
201-823-7252

Contains information on New Jersey, New York, Puerto Rico, Virgin Islands.

Pacific Northwest
6125 Sand Point Way NE
Seattle, WA 98115
206-526-6507

Contains information on Alaska, Idaho, Oregon, Washington state.

Pacific Sierra
1000 Commodore Drive
San Bruno, CA 94066
415-876-9009

Contains information on Hawaii, Nevada, northern California.

Pacific Southwest
24000 Avila Road
Mailing address: P.O. Box 6719
Laguna Niguel, CA 92677-6719
714-643-4241

Contains information on Arizona, southern California, Nevada's Clark County.

Rocky Mountain
Building 48, Denver Federal Center
Denver, CO 80225
303-236-0818

Contains information on Colorado, Montana, North Dakota, South Dakota, Utah, Wyoming.

Southwest
501 West Felix Street
Mailing address: P.O. Box 6216
Fort Worth, TX 76115
817-334-5525

Contains information on Arkansas, Louisiana, New Mexico, Oklahoma, Texas.

National Genealogical Society
4527 17th Street North
Arlington, VA 22207-02363

Request information on their genealogical forms and research aids, family group sheet, and newsletter.

National Union Catalog of Manuscript Collections.

A multivolume series with supplements. Available in larger libraries, it lists holdings of manuscripts under individual surnames. This work may tell you if any members of your family have papers deposited in a library or archive in this country.

New York Genealogical and Biographical Society
122 East 58th Street
New York, NY 10022
212-755-8532

Land records, probate records, Surrogate Court decisions. Includes materials on New England and the South.

New York Public Library
American History, Local History, and Genealogy Division
Fifth Avenue at 42nd Street, Room 315S
New York, NY 10036
212-930-0828

Published family histories, passenger lists, indexes to births and deaths, government records, including the census on microfilm.

Norlie, O. M. *Norwegian-American Papers, 1847–1946*. Northfield, MN: 1946.

Guide to Norwegian newspapers published in the United States.

Norwegian Tracks
Norwegian-American Genealogical Society
502 West Water Street
Decorah, IA 52101

A quarterly publication.

Olsson, Nils William. *Swedish Passenger Arrivals in New York 1820–1850.* **Chicago: Swedish Pioneer Historical Society, 1967.**

A highly specialized but invaluable resource. The passenger lists are organized chronologically and by name of vessel and point of departure, and register each passenger by name, age, sex, and profession. Annotations include any additional information available concerning the passengers. Often this information is extensive, tracing the immigrants' subsequent travels and careers. Also includes indexes of place names, personal names, and ships' names.

Peterson, Julius G. *Leafing out Your Swedish Family Tree.* **New York: Vantage Press, 1989.**

This book takes an unusual and sophisticated approach to genealogy, including chapters on "Bloodlines–Artificial Insemination," genetic markers, and the author's philosophy of life and genealogy. It is, nonetheless, an excellent place to begin research on your Swedish ancestry. In addition to chapters on methods and sources, it devotes a hundred pages to a general overview of Sweden: a chronology (covering 130 BC–AD 1981), a list of Swedish kings, an exploration of Swedish traditions and "The New Sweden." Bibliography and index.

Smith, Frank, and Thomsen, Finn A. *Genealogical Guidebook & Atlas of Denmark.* **Salt Lake City, UT: Bookcraft, 1969.**

Not a how-to book, but rather a guide to resources. Chapters on Danish words and their meanings, personal given names, the Gothic alphabet, converting the feast day calendar to the modern calendar, lists of parishes and place names, keyed to included maps.

Tepper, Michael. *American Passenger Records: A Guide to the Records of Immigrants Arriving at American Ports by Sail and Steam.* **Baltimore: Genealogical Publishing Co., 1993.**

Contains information on records from the colonial period to the beginning of mass immigration in the nineteenth and twentieth centuries. Several examples of passenger lists and how to read them. Appendix B contains a list of passenger list publications.

Thomsen, Finn A. *Scandinavian Genealogical Research Manual,* **3 vols. Bountiful, UT: Thomsen's Genealogical Center, 1980.**

Three volumes in one. Volume 1: Danish-Norwegian Guide and Dictionary. Volume 2: The Old Handwriting and Names of Denmark and Norway. Volume 3: Danish-Norwegian Genealogical Research Manual. Volumes 1 and 2, devoted to language and record interpretation, can be used in conjunction with volume 3, which is an extensive and detailed list of sources, together with information on how to use them. Volume 3 contains chapters on county, church, census, probate, and military records, as well as lists of important Danish and Norwegian sources and sources located at the Genealogical Society in Salt Lake City. Nine pages are devoted to research techniques. Includes a list of archives, libraries, and genealogical societies, with addresses. Bibliography.

Wellauer, Maralyn A. *Tracing Your Norwegian Roots.* **Author, 1979.**

A simplified guide, containing short but informative chapters on immigrants, pioneer life, the social order, and the Bygdelag Movement (immigrant social groups organized by Norwegian region of origin and operating around the turn of the century). Also includes maps and resource addresses, which should be double-checked, as this volume is now somewhat dated.

Westin, Jeane Eddy. *Finding Your Roots: How Every American Can Trace His Ancestors—At Home and Abroad.* **New York: Ballantine Books, 1977.**

Instructions on how to gather family records, using libraries and genealogical societies, local public records and federal records. Covers writing and publishing family history. Lists of archives and stores specializing in genealogical searches.

Where to Write for Vital Records: Births, Deaths, Marriages and Divorces.
Superintendent of Documents
U.S. Government Printing Office
Washington, DC 20402

An indispensable research guide.

SCANDINAVIAN GENEALOGICAL SOCIETIES

Bishop Hill Old Settlers Association
P.O. Box 68
Bishop Hill, IL 61419
309-927-3345
e-mail: webmaster@www.outfitters.com.

The Bishop Hill Colony was one of the most important forces in bringing Scandinavians to the United States. The association is currently compiling a list of the living direct descendants of the Bishop Hill Colony from 1846 to 1861.

Bygdelagenes Fellesraad Council
10129 Goodrich Circle
Bloomington, MN 55437
612-831-4409
e-mail: rmsylte@uci.edu

The council is made up of organizations formed by emigrant descendants from particular areas of Norway who are now living in North America. Each organization features its own newsletter that can be obtained for a minimal fee.

Danish-American Genealogical Group
c/o Minnesota Genealogy Society
P.O. Box 16069
Saint Paul, MN 55116-0069
612-645-3671
e-mail: mgsdec@mtn.org.

This is a subgroup of the Scandinavian-American Genealogical Society, and was founded in 1982. They hold monthly meetings to discuss Danish history, immigration, and the use of various Danish genealogical sources.

The Norwegian-American Historical Association
1510 St. Olaf Avenue
Northfield, MN 55057
507-646-3221
e-mail: webmaster@stolaf.edu

Strives to locate, collect, preserve, and interpret Norwegian American genealogical information. Has an extensive archive of genealogical data and has published over eighty different publications to date.

Swedish Genealogical Group
c/o Minnesota Genealogical Society
P.O. Box 16069
Saint Paul, MN 55116-0069
612-645-3671
e-mail: phyllis.pladsen@sparecom.mn.org.

Another subgroup of the Scandinavian American Genealogical Society, the Swedish Genealogical Group publishes a variety of materials on Swedish American genealogy. They also hold meetings four times a year.

Chapter 4
Oral History

Lisa Olson Paddock's first experience with oral history came at an early age, when she was eleven or twelve years old. Lisa was interested in discovering more about her Swedish grandfather's journey by freighter to America shortly after the turn of the century. Her grandfather was only thirteen at the time, Lisa knew, and it seemed strange that he would be traveling alone, working his way over by peeling vegetables to feed the ship's crew. Gradually, Lisa's grandfather began to tell his painful story: he had come, he said, to search for his mother, who had abandoned him when he was a toddler to come to the United States to seek her fortune. He never found his mother, but he did gain a new life in the New World, where he put his shipboard work experience to use by becoming a chef on the Union Pacific Railroad.

As this story illustrates, interviews or "oral histories" have the potential to fill gaps in your genealogical record that no amount of research could adequately explain. It also illustrates the fact that conducting such interviews can require a considerable amount of sensitivity. You will find after doing a few interviews that the psychology of interviewing can be mastered and that much of it is quite natural; it is what people do all the time in less formal contexts. Interviewing is simply a matter of cultivating social skills you already possess. You are sizing up a situation and deciding when to be tactful, when to be direct, when to push a point, when to back off. It may help to speak your interviewee's native tongue. You may not speak a Scandinavian language, but using certain words in the relevant language during the interview may help your interviewee open up—as might asking for the equivalents of certain English words.

Older relatives may be able to share stories and skills passed down through generations. Here, Peter Gross is shown practicing the traditional Norwegian craft of cabinetmaking.

You will notice that you may have to tailor your interviewing style to each interviewee. Some people like nothing better than talking about themselves and their families, and you may find that you have much more information than you can use. Other people might be more reluctant to share details of their lives. You will have to gain their trust. Be tactful when phrasing questions, and don't press an issue when the interviewee obviously does not want to address it. Most important, make sure you have done background work ahead of time. Gather documents and written statements before beginning oral history interviews. This way, if your interviewee gets sidetracked trying to remember when an event occurred, you will be able to supply the date by consulting your own notes. This will not only keep the conversation moving, it will also impress your interviewee with your preparedness.

Have a set of questions prepared before the interview begins. Make sure that your questions are open-ended and require more than a yes-or-no answer. This will help to get the interviewee into the flow of conversation. Try to create a comfortable, quiet environment for the interview, with no interruptions or phone calls. The more private your conversation, the more forthcoming your interviewee is likely to be.

Your first set of questions should clarify basic facts about the interviewee, such as his or her birthdate, place of birth, present occupation, place of residence, and marital status. You might find some surprises even in answers to these simple questions. When Lisa asked her grandfather where he was born, he told her that because he was born on the ferry that connects Helsingborg, Sweden, with Helsingor, Denmark, he was not entirely certain whether he was officially Swedish or Danish.

Now start to dig a little deeper. Try to get the interviewee to talk about his or her own family history: parents, grandparents, great-grandparents, or as far back as he or she can remember. What does he or she know about the family's settlement in the United States and their lives here?

It was not until she was preparing to write this book that

Ask your interviewees whether their political affiliations have ever been influenced by their Scandinavian American backgrounds. Henry Jackson, the late Democratic congressman from Washington who campaigned for the presidential nomination in 1972 and 1976, was of Swedish descent.

Lisa discovered that her grandfather's experience was part of a larger pattern of Swedish migration to America: around 1890, it changed abruptly because of improved conditions in Scandinavia, and the rate of family emigration began to fall while that of single individuals rose. If she had known this in advance, her discussion with her grandfather might have resulted in both parties having learned something valuable— the mark of a truly successful interview.

Be sure to get as complete a picture of your interviewee as you can. What other jobs has he or she held? Is he or she involved in any other activities? Narrow down details of your interviewee's educational background, political affiliations, and religious beliefs. Has he or she had any involvement in the Scandinavian American community?

If the interview is being conducted in your interviewee's home, you might ask whether he or she has any materials such as trophies, photos, certificates, diplomas, or personal records that you might examine. If the interview is held at your home or at another location, ask in advance that the interviewee bring along any items he or she would like to talk about or that he or she feels are particularly relevant to the family history.

Always tape-record the interview, if possible. It is easy to miss important details when you are trying to take notes. You want to be able to concentrate on what the interviewee is saying, not on your own notebook. Always be sure to tell the interviewee that you would like to tape-record the interview. He or she will probably be nervous about being recorded at first, but will probably forget that the recorder is even there.

Allow your interviewee to talk at his or her own pace. Don't force questions or ask too many questions at once. Never interrupt your interviewee. If you have an idea of something to say, make a note of it. If there is a lull in the conversation later on, your comments may help your interviewee think of additional information.

There may be interviews in which you will need to get the interviewee interested and excited about your discussion by telling him or her some things you have already learned about your family or about Scandinavia in general. A reluctant or quiet interviewee may catch your enthusiasm and open up.

Interviews by Mail

If the relatives you wish to contact live far away from you, you may want to reach them by mail. The first thing to do when attempting to contact relatives by mail is to write a good cover letter. Included with the cover letter should be a list of questions you would like them to answer, copies of your partially completed pedigree charts and family group sheets, and a self-addressed, stamped envelope.

It is important that the cover letter be both direct and personal. A well-written, polite cover letter will catch someone's attention and reduce the chance that your letter will be discarded along with the junk mail. You could use the following letter as a model for your cover letter, or you could consult another source listed at the end of this chapter.

Dear _____:

My name is _____, and I am conducting a research project on the _____ family. I was hoping you could take the time to answer the enclosed list of questions and fill out any information you can on the enclosed pedigree chart. Also, please let me know of any errors you might notice on the chart. When you have finished, please send me the question sheet, pedigree chart, and any other information or questions you may wish to include in the self-addressed envelope that I have enclosed.

I would also be grateful if you could let me know if anyone else in the family is doing genealogical research that would help me in my project, or if you know anyone else who would be willing to contribute information or memories. Any such information would be a great help.

When I have finished my research I would be more than happy to share the results with you. Please let me know if you want me to send a copy to you.

Thank you very much for your time and assistance, and I hope to hear from you soon.

Sincerely,

[your signature]

The questions you send should be general, allowing your relative the freedom to take the answer wherever he or she chooses. Refrain from asking questions that are presumptuous or potentially offensive. Here are some sample questions to start with, but you will probably want to come up with some of your own.

- What was your childhood like? What was your school experience like? What were your hobbies and interests? What was your family and home life like? Do you have any memorable anecdotes you could share with me about your childhood?
- Did you go to college? If so, what was it like? Were you married? What was your wedding like? What kind of job(s) did you have? Were you ever in the military? Did you take any memorable vacations?
- What historic events stand out in your mind? How did they affect your life at that time? What changes have you witnessed in economics, technology, politics, or fashion?
- Do you know any Scandinavian myths, legends, songs, or folktales? Have you ever participated in any traditional ceremonies or holidays? If so, please explain.
- Are you aware of the location of any personal papers, bibles, or diaries belonging to family members? Do you know of any photographs or illustrations of our ancestors? Do you know of anyone in the family who has already done genealogical research?

After the Interview

Short follow-up conversations on the phone or in person may

be necessary after the interview. Always write a thank-you letter after the interview; mention that you may have more questions later. Offer to share the results of the interview, ask for help in correcting any mistakes, and ask whether your interviewee has found any new documents or pictures.

Although it can be quite tedious and time-consuming to transcribe, or write up, your interviews, it is the best way to evaluate all of the information you have received. You may even find that looking at the full transcript of the interview gives you ideas on how to structure your family history.

You can also conduct interviews through the mail. Older family members in particular might enjoy corresponding with you, and communicating by mail will certainly be less expensive than making long-distance calls. Write a short letter asking a few pertinent questions. You might want to format these questions into a questionnaire that your relatives could simply fill out and return to you. To make things even easier for them, enclose a self-addressed stamped envelope. Even if your letters are not answered, follow up with a phone call; your relatives have probably thought about your questions even if they have not had time to respond.

If you have access to electronic mail (e-mail), you may actually be able to form a circle of correspondents willing to handle your questions and provide advice or information. This form of communication will add an immediacy and excitement to your search.

Interviewing can be enjoyable and interesting. Interviewees often emerge from the exercise saying they never knew intervewing could be so much fun. Your interviewee may be inspired to look for new information. You will not only gain valuable data for your project, but may form new connections with family members as well.

Resources

ORAL HISTORY

Allen, Barbara, and Montell, William Lynwood. *From Memory to History: Using Oral Sources in Local Historical Research*. Nashville, TN: American Association for State and Local History, 1981.

> Particularly stimulating reading for researchers who have assembled an archive of oral histories and wish to write a family or public history based on the material. See especially Chapter 6: "Producing a Manuscript from Oral Sources."

Bremmer, Robert H., ed. *Essays on History and Literature*. Columbus: Ohio State University Press, 1966.

> See Daniel Aaron's essay, "The Treachery of Recollection: The Inner and the Outer History," for an informative discussion of ways historians treat contemporary history and living memory.

Davis, Cullom; Back, Kathryn; and Maclean, Kay. *Oral History: From Tape to Type*. Chicago: American Library Association, 1977.

> Chapters on collecting oral history, interviewing, transcribing, editing. Glossary and bibliography. Several illustrations of how to organize interviews, do cross-referencing, and take notes.

Deering, Mary Jo, and Pomeroy, Barbara. *Transcribing without Tears: A Guide to Transcribing and Editing Oral History Interviews*. Washington, DC: Oral History Program, George Washington University Library, 1976.

How to deal with problems such as overlapping speech, syntax, inaccuracies, false starts, dangling sentences, fuzzy thinking, paragraphing. How to use editing symbols such as ellipses, dashes, brackets, and footnotes.

Degh, Linda; Glassie, Henry; and Oinas, Felix J. *Folklore Today*. Bloomington: Indiana University Press, 1976.

In "Legend: Oral Tradition in the Modern Experience," William Hugh Janson provides insights into how oral narratives are constructed by both those telling the story and those listening to it. Although this is an article meant for scholars, it is worth studying because it reveals how families and other groups shape their history.

Evans, George Ewart. *Spoken History*. London: Faber and Faber, 1987.

In Chapter 2, "The Interview," Evans discusses what it is like to interview people not accustomed to tape recorders.

Garner, Van Hastings. *Oral History: A New Experience in Learning*. Dayton, OH: Pflaum Publishing, 1975.

Chapters on equipment, how to set up interviews, organization of the interview, technique, and style. Bibliography.

Harris, Ramon, et al. *The Practice of Oral History*. Glen Rock, NJ: Microfilming Corporation of America, 1975.

Chapters on preparing for interviews, processing and editing interviews, present and future uses of oral history. See also appendixes: helpful hints for interviewers, samples of logbook form, and other archival forms.

Hoopes, James. *Oral History: An Introduction for Students*. Chapel Hill: University of North Carolina Press, 1979.

Chapters on arranging, preparing, and conducting interviews, and on how to use interview material for papers. A listing of oral history collections and sources, bibliography.

Ives, Edward I. *The Tape-Recorded Interview: A Manual for Field Workers in Folklore and Oral History*. **Knoxville: University of Tennessee Press, 1974.**

While the discussion of tape recorders may be outdated, other chapters will be of interest, such as those on interviewing techniques and how to make a transcript of the interview. The appendix includes a compendium of forms used by the Northeast Archives of Folklore and Oral History. Also included are illustrations of edited oral history transcripts, letters to interviewees, and release forms (used for getting permission to use interviewees' remarks). Brief bibliography.

Jorgensen, Danny L. *Participant Observation: A Methodology for Human Studies*. **Newbury Park, CA: Sage Publications, 1989.**

See Chapters 6, 7, and 8 for a discussion of interviewing, recordkeeping, and ways of reconstructing what you learn from your interviews and observations. Bibliography.

McGoldrick, Monica, and Gerson, Randy. *Genograms in Family Assessment*. **New York: W. W. Norton, 1985.**

See Chapter 5 for an explanation of the genogram interview and for suggestions on how to ask sensitive questions.

Meckler, Alan M., and McMullin, Ruth. *Oral History Collections*. **New York: R. R. Bowker, 1975.**

Divided into a name and subject index. Listings for individuals, states, and organizations. Separate sections on U.S. and foreign oral history centers.

Schumacher, Michael. *Creative Conversations: The Writer's Complete Guide to Conducting Interviews*. **Cincinnati: Writer's Digest Books, 1990.**

See especially the first chapter, "The Interview and Its Uses." Although this is a book for professional writers, it contains many useful tips for the family historian and genealogist.

Terkel, Studs. *Hard Times: An Oral History of the Depression*. New York: Avon Books, 1971.

A popular oral historian, Terkel provides a good model of how to shape and organize oral history interviews. Pay close attention to the way he structures his book, emphasizing the themes that arise out of his interviewees' recollections.

Thompson, Paul. *The Voice of the Past: Oral History*. New York: Oxford University Press, 1978.

Explores the method and meaning of oral history. See especially the chapter on "the interview," which gives helpful tips on sequencing and phrasing questions. Includes model questions for the oral history interview.

Tonkin, Elizabeth. *Narrating Our Pasts: The Social Construction of Oral History*. Cambridge: Cambridge University Press, 1992.

A difficult book for advanced readers interested in the questions oral history raises: how truthful are oral accounts of the past, and to what extent can we rely on autobiographies? Bibliography.

Vansina, Jan. *Oral Tradition as History*. Madison: University of Wisconsin Press, 1985.

For advanced readers wishing to explore interpretation of oral histories. Even beginners, however, will profit from the first chapter's discussion of the different kinds of evidence to be found in oral history interviews and the oral tradition. See also the last chapter, which assesses the strengths and limitations of the oral tradition.

Chapter 5
Making a Scandinavian American Family History

What kind of family history interests you? Do you want to compile a complete record of the family, including a genealogical chart or outline, a family tree that will be handed on to subsequent generations of your family? Or are you concentrating on a few generations, including colorful stories and anecdotes that might interest not only your family but your friends, or even a larger audience? (If you are thinking of publishing your history, consult the **Resources** section for Kirk Polking's book, *Writing Family Histories and Memoirs*.)

In the course of your research, you may discover that you are the product of a multiethnic heritage. Will this fact be the focus of your history? In the United States, it has always been an open question as to how much an immigrant group must absorb of the prevailing culture. Should the children of immigrants retain their parents' language? Should that language be taught in school? How has your family reacted to these questions? Has it consciously tried to preserve its Scandinavian roots? Or has it conformed with the tradition of the "melting pot," in which different ethnic groups are envisioned as forming a new nation of Americans, as described in Crevecoeur's *Letters of an American Farmer*.

Inevitably, raising such questions will tell you something about your family's reaction to becoming American, and the story of what America means will become a part of your family history.

If one special ancestor interests you, your family history will become an exercise in biography. (For the literature on this subject, see Carl Rollyson, *Biography: An Annotated*

As you write your family history, you might include colorful details about traditional Scandinavian holidays or celebrations your family has maintained. The Santa Lucia festival, Sweden's traditional festival of lights, involves the crowning of a young woman with a ring of candles.

Bibliography. Englewood Cliffs, NJ: Salem Press, 1993.) A family member, stimulated by your research, may ask you to help create a family history or a reminiscence. Here, oral history tapes will be most helpful. You may want to transcribe and edit certain sections, asking your interviewee for more commentary, introductions, conclusions, and asking other family members to contribute their thoughts as well. The result will be a unique family album based on one individual's experiences.

How you decide on the form of your family history will depend on your interests, obviously, but it will also depend on how much time you have to devote to the project and on the kinds of data you are able to obtain. Some family histories entail traveling; others might be done, in part, by telephone and correspondence.

Of course, what you write is a personal history even if you are not writing about yourself. Why you choose to write about your grandfather rather than your grandmother, or your aunt instead of your uncle, or your brother instead of your sister, may say a great deal about your family relationships. You may decide to write about a family member you know extremely well, or perhaps about a relative who is something of a mystery to you.

In any case, think about the audience for your family history. Is it for yourself, for school, for your family in general, for one particular relative? How you write and assemble your family history will depend on these factors and others.

Do not be surprised if the shape of your family history changes as you continue to research and write. You may have in mind one kind of family history, only to find in writing it that you are doing something quite different. Be prepared to revise your plans; such changes can be a great part of the excitement of doing family history. It is also possible that you will have enough material for more than one kind of family history, so that you become a historian, a biographer, a genealogist, and even an autobiographer.

Perhaps you want to tell your own story in the context of your family history. See the **Resources** section at the end of this chapter and Chapter 2 for examples of autobiography and journal writing. Some autobiographies are straightforward and chronological, while others may be organized by topic or may focus on a few specific events.

You might choose to organize your family history in a scrapbook. Create a collage of pictures, documents, and other papers, tying them together with your own commentary. You might caption photos or documents with quotes from older relatives, perhaps describing the old country or memories of their early experiences as Americans.

Pedigree Charts and Family Group Sheets

There are a variety of forms you can buy to help you organize important information about your family. You can obtain these forms in a number of different ways. The easiest, but also the most expensive, way to get genealogical forms is from a genealogical supplier. You will find the addresses for a few of these companies at the end of this chapter. Another way to get the charts is to go to a research library with a genealogical section and pay twenty-five to fifty cents for a copy of each form you need. Then you can photocopy them when you need them. Lastly, and least expensively, you can create your own forms based on an example in a genealogy book.

The most commonly used forms in family research are family group sheets and pedigree charts. They provide a way to access quickly and easily information that you have gathered in notebooks or other sheets of paper. Take copies of your family group sheets and pedigree charts when you go to research so that you can quickly decide what information you have and what you lack. Also, these charts are a great way to share your genealogical findings with other researchers in your extended family. You can find examples of these forms on the following pages.

Family group sheets, as the name suggests, contain the genealogical information for an individual family or couple. They usually include the name, date of birth, and place of birth for each member of a nuclear family. When filling out a family group sheet, include information for each member of that immediate family, whether they lived together or not. Also included are the date of marriage for the parents and, if necessary, the date of death and place of burial for any deceased members. Should either of the parents have remarried, the data for that family would occupy a separate sheet.

Pedigree charts bring together the information from all your family group sheets. In a sense, the pedigree charts serve as an enormous family tree, extending from your earliest known ancestor all the way through to the current generation. But unlike the family trees you have seen, the pedigree charts are usually laid out horizontally, proceeding from left to right, from the past to the present. Also, pedigree charts usually contain more data than family trees.

Pedigree Chart

Name of Compiler _____

Address _____

City, State _____

Date _____

Person No.1 on this chart is the same person as No.____on chart No.____.

Chart No.____

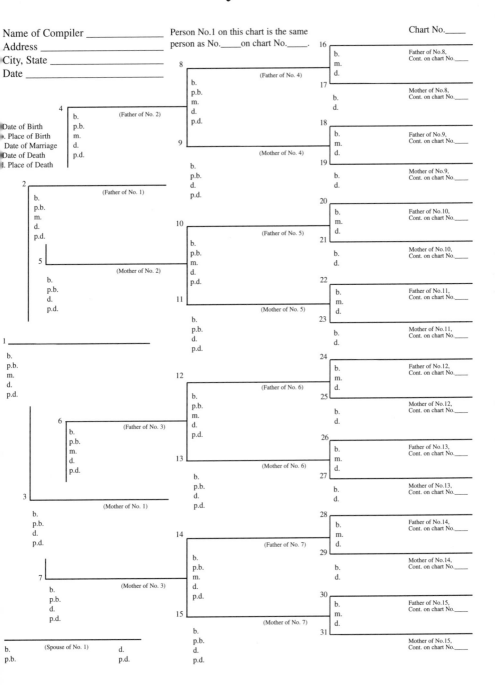

4

Date of Birth
Place of Birth
Date of Marriage
Date of Death
Place of Death

8   (Father of No. 4)
b.
p.b.
m.
d.
p.d.

(Father of No. 2)
b.
p.b.
m.
d.
p.d.

9   (Mother of No. 4)
b.
p.b.
d.
p.d.

16
b.
m.
d.
Father of No.8,
Cont. on chart No.____

17
b.
d.
Mother of No.8,
Cont. on chart No.____

18
b.
m.
d.
Father of No.9,
Cont. on chart No.____

19
b.
d.
Mother of No.9,
Cont. on chart No.____

2   (Father of No. 1)
b.
p.b.
m.
d.
p.d.

10   (Father of No. 5)
b.
p.b.
m.
d.
p.d.

5
b.
p.b.
d.
p.d.

(Mother of No. 2)

11   (Mother of No. 5)
b.
p.b.
d.
p.d.

20
b.
m.
d.
Father of No.10,
Cont. on chart No.____

21
b.
d.
Mother of No.10,
Cont. on chart No.____

22
b.
m.
d.
Father of No.11,
Cont. on chart No.____

23
b.
d.
Mother of No.11,
Cont. on chart No.____

1 _____
b.
p.b.
m.
d.
p.d.

12   (Father of No. 6)
b.
p.b.
m.
d.
p.d.

6   (Father of No. 3)
b.
p.b.
m.
d.
p.d.

13   (Mother of No. 6)
b.
p.b.
d.
p.d.

24
b.
m.
d.
Father of No.12,
Cont. on chart No.____

25
b.
d.
Mother of No.12,
Cont. on chart No.____

26
b.
m.
d.
Father of No.13,
Cont. on chart No.____

27
b.
d.
Mother of No.13,
Cont. on chart No.____

3
b.
p.b.
d.
p.d.

(Mother of No. 1)

7   (Mother of No. 3)
b.
p.b.
d.
p.d.

14   (Father of No. 7)
b.
p.b.
m.
d.
p.d.

15   (Mother of No. 7)
b.
p.b.
d.
p.d.

28
b.
m.
d.
Father of No.14,
Cont. on chart No.____

29
b.
d.
Mother of No.14,
Cont. on chart No.____

30
b.
m.
d.
Father of No.15,
Cont. on chart No.____

31
b.
d.
Mother of No.15,
Cont. on chart No.____

(Spouse of No. 1)
b.
p.b.
d.
p.d.

FAMILY GROUP WORK SHEET #_____

HUSBAND, Name:		WIFE, Name:	
Birth:	Place:	Birth:	Place:
Death:	Place:	Death:	Place:
Burial:	Place:	Burial:	Place:
Father:		Father:	
Mother:		Mother:	
Occupation:		Occupation:	
Notes:		Notes:	

Name	Date & Place of Birth	Date & Place of Marriage	Date & Place of Death	Married to	Date & Place of Birth	Death

Although both family group sheets and pedigree charts are a concise and highly organized way to store genealogical data, they should never take the place of personal notes or copies of documents. It is always a good idea to keep your notes and documents on file along with your family group sheets and pedigree charts. This way you have a back-up copy against which you can verify any questionable information on the charts, without losing the accessibility of the charts.

A trip to Scandinavia might be a long-term goal of your family history project. Perhaps you can visit your family's hometown or even visit living relatives who live in Scandinavia. Even if such a trip is impossible, you can continue to follow current events in your family's native country by reading newspaper or magazine articles. You might look up the ancestral village in a country travel guide, for example, to see how it might have changed today. If you are going to make a trip to Scandinavia, read as much as you can about the history and culture of the country you will be visiting before your trip.

A good place to begin is with the books listed in the **Resources** sections of Chapters 1 and 2 that concern the history and culture of the various Scandinavian countries. One way to approach your historical and cultural studies would be to work backward in time, essentially reversing your ancestor's experiences. Ole Edvart Rölvaag's epic trilogy *Giants of the Earth* (1927), *Peder Victorious* (1929), and *Their Father's God* (1931), concerning the trials of Norwegian immigrants to the Dakotas and based on Rölvaag's own experiences, will give you a sense of how a Scandinavian sensibility reacted to the New World. The same mixture of realism and mysticism that marks Rölvaag's work also characterizes another set of epic novels written by a Norwegian. Sigrid Undset's trilogy *Kristin Lavransdatter*, set in fourteenth-century Norway, presents a vivid picture of life in medieval Scandinavia and provides an instructive contrast with Rölvaag's nineteenth-century saga. The significance of the saga form—as illustrated by, say, the Icelandic Snorri Sturluson's history of Norway, *Heimskringla*—in Scandinavian literature cannot be overestimated. Through such works you can learn a great deal about both Scandinavian history and sensibilities.

Finland, long dominated by Sweden and Swedish culture, did not have its own written language until the sixteenth century. You can find a history of Finland's legendary past in its national epic, the *Kalevala*, a collection of folk poetry passed down through the generations by word of mouth and first published in 1835.

Consulting these Scandinavian texts will give you a sense of the richness of Scandinavian history and the sophistication and creativity with which it has been documented. By compiling your own family history, you are making your own voice heard. In the process, you will learn not only about your past, but also about your future as you continue to explore your Scandinavian American identity.

Creating a Family Tree

As the term suggests, family trees show the branches of a family. The most common form of the family tree is a genealogical chart showing several generations of a family. Most books devoted to genealogy have examples of such charts. Often biographers put them at the beginning of their books, so that readers can clearly follow the bloodlines of a family. With large families it is easy to get lost in the names of all the relatives—some of them repeated over the generations. A family tree systematizes the relationships.

A family tree can also be used as a basis for further research. It will help you to see where the gaps are. You may have the name of a great-grandfather but be missing your great-grandmother's name, or her date of birth, or her country of origin. You can still make a place for that relative in your family tree, putting question marks next to gaps in information. Thus a partial birthdate might be listed as 189? or c. 1890s (when you know the decade or period but really don't have a specific date). Perhaps you can gradually narrow the gap, later writing in 1892–94?

A family tree helps to visualize a family's history. It can be done as a graphic, so that it actually looks like a tree, with branches extending both into the past and into the future. But a family tree can also be a kind of outline, the first generation represented by a Roman numeral I, the second generation as II, and so on. The outline form allows you to incorporate more information, and it can be revised quite easily, especially if you are using a word processor. You can include not only dates of births and deaths, marriages, and other significant events, but also descriptions of places where your family members settled and worked.

Another possibility is to combine the graphic and outline forms of the family tree. If you are using a word processor, you can turn the graphic family tree into a modified outline by using the footnote key. After recording the important dates for, say, your grandfather, you could footnote him— that is, insert a note at the bottom of the page giving details of his life and family history. Footnotes might also be the place to indicate gaps in your information. Perhaps you want to know why your grandparents moved from rural Nebraska to Chicago. Put this question in your footnote so that you can follow it up in library research or interviews.

One model of the family tree is given in Oscar Lewis's *The Children of Sanchez*. Notice how he makes the family progenitor (head of the family) the center of the tree but also uses several different symbols to indicate parents and children, marriage bonds, siblings with different fathers, and the order of marriages. The tree provides a concentrated picture of family relationships and makes their complications clear and easy to follow. For other examples of family trees, consult the **Resources** section of this chapter.

Think of the family tree as your family's skeletal structure. It delineates basic relationships. It also maps your family's movements. The family tree is the foundation on which you can erect a full family history. The next chapter provides several examples of what might be called family history extensions of the family tree. How you develop the tree depends greatly on your personality and interests. It may serve as the basis of your autobiography. It may be used to introduce a family scrapbook of reminiscences and documents. It could serve to clarify relationships for readers of your family's oral history.

The family tree is both a starting and an ending point. Do not be discouraged if there are gaps in the tree—branches of the family or details about your progenitor and his or her descendants that are missing. Other family members may eventually discover new information—sometimes literally

Your family tree should include a detailed description of your progenitor, including an account of his or her occupation. Here, Norwegian American Christian Hauge worked as a foreman of steel erection in 1949.

digging it up out of old trunks and boxes of long-forgotten papers. The tree itself establishes the importance of your family history and may well stimulate family discussion that contributes additional data.

Whatever shape your family tree ultimately takes (and it may change several times before you find a format that suits you), you should begin assembling the tree by concentrating on your family progenitor or emigrant ancestor—that is, the grandparent, great-grandparent, or great-great-grandparent from whom you trace your family's Scandinavian American roots. Although Scandinavian ethnic groups are patrilineal, you may be tracing your lineage through either a male or female ancestor. Write a paragraph giving the progenitor's dates of birth and death, his or her parentage (if known), and your sources for this information. Then start another paragraph, specifying the progenitor's date and place of marriage (or approximate dates and the sources on which you base your statement). Give the spouse's full name and parentage, as well as the dates of birth and death. List other facts that reveal his or her origins and life history. Was he or she married before? Did he or she have children by a previous marriage? Do you know their names? You may need to write additional paragraphs, depending on how many children and marriages are involved in the progenitor's generation. If your progenitor was married several times, write a separate paragraph on the facts of each marriage.

Establish as clearly as possible what you know about your progenitor and his or her spouse and how you know it. Other family members may be able to add to or correct this record once they see it set down, and your account may prove helpful to another family historian at a later time.

With the facts clearly established, write an account of your progenitor's life, beginning with details such as place of birth or first memories. Then explain what you know about his or her schooling, military service, jobs or offices held, travels—all the details that will fill out a picture of his or her life. Include reminiscences about him or her obtained in oral history interviews or in letters. If he or she left a will, that too may say something about the kind of person he or she was.

Consider adding material about Scandinavia and about immigration to this country from the history and literature books you have read. You may begin to see how your family fits into the great movement of people to a new land. If you do refer to material you have read, be certain to specify your sources—the author, title, publisher, and date of the work you have relied upon, and the page number on which the material appears.

Computer Genealogy

Genealogical research has come a long way since the days of your ancestors. Family research has traditionally been done by hand, but with the advent of new technology comes a new day for the preparation and display of genealogical information.

Many family historians use word processing computer programs to prepare their written histories. These programs are preferable to typewriters because you can correct, move, and alter text with far greater ease.

Aside from word processing, computers are becoming an even greater assistance to family historians. Software is constantly being developed to simplify every aspect of genealogical research.

The Personal Ancestral File (PAF), created by the Church of Jesus Christ of Latter-day Saints, is one of the finest programs available for genealogical work. Developed in response to the enormous amounts of data collected each year, this program goes through continual revisions to keep it up to date. The Family Records program of the PAF allows you to input your genealogical data, and it organizes the data for you. You can also print out the information in family group or pedigree chart formats.

Many other companies have developed similar software for genealogists. In fact, you can often find collections of censuses, vital record indexes, and prepared family histories—information that was once restricted to the library—available on CD-ROM. Most of these programs are now available for both Macintosh and IBM and compatible personal computers computers.

When shopping for genealogical programs, look for software with the GEDCOM format. GEDCOM (Genealogical Data Communications) is a file format that allows running files and information from one program in GEDCOM format to another. This capability makes sharing data with fellow researchers very easy. It will also let you move information to an entirely different program (provided it is also a GEDCOM program), should you decide to do so.

In addition to the organizational and word processing benefits of computer genealogy, almost every genealogical software program includes an output function that allows you to print out pre-formatted pedigree charts, family group sheets, and, most important, family trees. If you have a scanner at home, or have access to one, you can scan in photos and other images. Software programs will incorporate these images into your family tree. Combine this capability with a high-quality laser printer and you will have a pleasing format to display your findings. Technology can assist in every aspect of your genealogical project—from data entry to creating a finished project.

Resources

AUTOBIOGRAPHY

Lagerlöf, Selma. *Mårbacka.* **Garden City, NY: Doubleday Doran, 1924.**

A volume of Lagerlöf's autobiography dealing with her parents, brothers and sisters, family servants, and with the people on whom some of the characters in her fiction were based.

————. *Memories of My Childhood: Further Years at Mårbacka.* **Garden City, NY: Doubleday Doran, 1934.**

Lewis, Oscar. *The Children of Sanchez: Autobiography of a Mexican Family.* **New York: Random House, 1961.**

This book, based on an anthropologist's study, can serve as one kind of model for a family tree and history. It begins and ends with the voice of Jesus Sanchez, the family progenitor, and in between devotes chapters to individual family members.

————. *A Death in the Sanchez Family.* **New York: Random House, 1969.**

A classic family history by a distinguished anthropologist. Made up exclusively of edited oral histories, this book is a model to be carefully studied for methods of shaping and presenting family history.

Padover, Saul K., ed. *Confessions and Self-Portraits: 4600 Years of Autobiography.* **New York: The John Day Company, 1957.**

A comprehensive selection of authors that depicts the many different forms of autobiography.

Sandburg, Carl. *Always the Young Strangers*. New York: Harcourt, Brace, 1953.

The famous American poet's autobiography, the only work in which he describes his upbringing by Swedish immigrant parents.

THE FAMILY IN SCANDINAVIA AND THE UNITED STATES

Davidson, H. R. Ellis. *Pagan Scandinavia*. New York: Praeger, 1967.

Includes a chapter on the family.

Foote, Peter G., and Wilson, David M. *The Viking Achievement: A Survey of the Society and Culture of Early Medieval Scandinavia*. New York: Praeger, 1970.

This study of medieval Scandinavian culture contains a chapter on women and marriage.

Frykman, Jonas, and Lofgren, Orvar. *Culture Builders: A Historical Anthropology of Middle-Class Life*. New Brunswick, NJ: Rutgers University Press, 1987.

A fascinating but advanced cultural study, with chapters on the Scandinavian sense of time, nature, the home, the "Cultural Basis of Physical Aversion," "Peasant View of Purity and Dirt," and "Bourgeois Discipline." Notes and bibliography.

Harris, C. C., ed. *Readings in Kinship in Urban Society*. New York: Pergamon Press, 1970.

See the essay on "Relations Between Generations and the Three-Generation Household in Denmark."

Hellstrom, Gustaf. *Lacemaker Lekholm Has an Idea*. New York: The Dial Press, 1931.

Follows three generations of a family, its successes and failures.

Kallberg, Sture. *Off the Middle Way: Report from a Swedish Village.* **New York: Pantheon Books, 1972.**

A study of different generations in a Swedish village and their everyday life. Contains much interesting firsthand testimony.

Kihlman, Christer. *The Blue Mother.* **Lincoln: University of Nebraska Press, 1990.**

This novel concentrates on the childhood of two brothers, revealing the explosive human emotions suppressed beneath their superficial respectability. The author is a strong critic of the conventions of Finnish society.

Mosk, Carl. *Patriarchy and Fertility: Japan and Sweden, 1880–1960.* **New York: Academic Press, 1983.**

Covers both urban and rural life, with tables, illustrations, and notes.

Myrdal, Alva Reimer. *Nation and Family: The Swedish Experiment in Democratic Family and Population Policy.* **New York: Harper & Brothers, 1941.**

Tables and diagrams.

Ramsoy, Natalie Rogoff, ed. *Norwegian Society.* **New York: Humanities Press, 1974.**

Chapters on population, the Norwegian family, kinship, and marriage.

Scott, Hilda. *Sweden's "Right to Be Human": Sex-Role Equality: The Goal and the Reality.* **Armonk, NY: M. E. Sharpe, 1982.**

Essays on equality, unionism, the family as individuals, education, the environment. Indexes of names and subjects.

Simpson, Jacqueline. *The Viking World.* **New York: St. Martin's Press, 1980.**

Chapters on family and society.

Singleton, Fred. *A Short History of Finland.*
Cambridge: Cambridge University Press, 1989.

A chapter on family life.

Tomasson, Richard F. *Sweden: Prototype of Modern Society.* New York: Random House, 1970.

Chapters on men, women, and the family.

FAMILY TREES AND FAMILY HISTORY

National Genealogical Society
4527 17th Street North
Arlington, VA 22207-02363

Request information on their genealogical forms and research aids, family group sheet, and newsletter.

Polking, Kirk. *Writing Family Histories and Memoirs.*
Cincinnati: Writer's Digest Press, 1995.

Chapters on how to begin writing a family history (involving your family, getting help from others, learning how to write dialogue), ideas for topics, becoming the family historian, where to find things in libraries, courthouses, electronic search services, tips on interviewing, different methods of organization, format and writing style, editing and publishing a manuscript. Bibliography.

Rye, Walter. *Records and Record Searching*, 2d ed.
Baltimore: Genealogical Publishing Co., 1969. [First published in 1897.]

See Chapter 1, how to compile a pedigree.

PEDIGREE CHARTS AND FAMILY GROUP SHEETS

Evelyn Spears Family Group Sheet Exchange
East 12502 Frideger Street
Elk, WA 99009

This service offers previously researched family group sheets for the surname you request. They charge approximately $10 per surname from a catalog of 14,000 surnames.

Schreiner-Yantis Family Group Sheets.

Family group sheets designed by Netti Schreiner-Yantis are considered the best on the market. You can write for a price list for the group sheets, as well as pedigree charts and other forms, at: GBIP, 6818 Lois Drive, Springfield, VA 22150.

FAMILY HISTORY ON COMPUTER

American Genealogical Lending Library (AGLL)
801-298-5446

This number allows you to access the AGLL electronic databases by phone. They also sell a few censuses on CD-ROM and marriage records on floppy disk.

Ancestral File Operations Unit
50 East North Temple Street
Salt Lake City, UT 84150
801-240-2584

Write or call for information on the Family History Library's Personal Ancestral File (PAF) software and the GEDCOM compatibility system.

Banner Blue Software
P.O. Box 7865
Fremont, CA 94537
510-795-4490

Banner Blue's Biography Maker software is designed to narrow your focus as you write your family history. This program also lets you write individual stories and combine them with history aids. Write for information.

Clifford, Karen. *Genealogy and Computers for the Complete Beginner*. **Baltimore: Genealogical Publishing Co., 1992.**

This text teaches beginning genealogists to apply new concepts to their research through exercises and quizzes.

Commsoft, Inc.
7795 Bell Road
P.O. Box 310
Windsor, CA 95495-0130

The Roots IV program has an extremely flexible data entry program that makes compiling and accessing data simple. Write for information.

Dollarhide Systems
203 Holly Street
Bellingham, WA 28225
801-298-5358

The Everyone's Family Tree program by Dollarhide is geared for beginners in genealogical research. Write for information.

Genealogical Computing

This periodical from Ancestry Publishing in Salt Lake City, contains the most current information on technology in ancestry hunting.

Interlock Software Systems
P.O. Box 130953
Houston, TX 77219
713-680-8576

Write for information on Generations Library Software.

LDB Association Inc.
Dept. Q, Box 20837
Wichita, KS 67208-6837
316-683-6200

Write for information on KinWrite and KinPublish software.

Quinsept, Inc.
P.O. Box 216
Lexington, MA 02173
1-800-637-ROOT

Call (toll-free) or write for information on Family Roots and Lineage software programs.

The Internet

A variety of services are available on the Internet for everyone from the beginner to the pro. There are chat boards, troubleshooting forums, and home pages for specific genealogical groups. You can ask your librarian for help if you have never used the Internet.

INTERNET WEB SITES
Everton Publishers Genealogy Page
http://www.everton.com

This page contains information on getting started as well as specific information on ethnic, religious, and social groups. Includes an online edition of the genealogical magazine *Everton's Genealogical Helper* and provides links to archives, libraries, and other Internet resources.

Genealogy Home Page
ftp://ftp.cac.psu.edu/pub/genealogy
http://ftp.cac.psu.edu/~saw/genealogy.html

By filling out the survey linked to this home page, you will be granted access to many genealogical links, allowing you to communicate with other genealogists, search new databases, and order genealogical software online.

LDS Research Guides
ftp://hipp.etsu.edu/pub/genealogy

This site focuses on the Research Outline Guides produced by the Family History Library in Salt Lake City. Subjects include getting started, frequently asked genealogy questions, and techniques for photograph dating.

National Archives and Records Administration
gopher://gopher.nara.gov
http://www.nara.gov

> NARA is the government agency responsible for managing the records of the federal government. Through this page you can find the location and business hours for regional archives or access information on finding and using particular government documents.

U.S. Census Bureau
ftp://gateway.census.gov
http://www.census.gov

> From this site you can find statistics about population, housing, economy, and geography as compiled by the U.S. Department of Commerce Bureau of the Census. You can also do sepcific word searches according to subject or geographic location.

World Wide Web Genealogy Demo Page
http://demo.genweb.org/gene/genedemo.html

> This page is still under construction, but its goal is to "create a coordinated, interlinked, distributed worldwide genealogy database." Even in its incomplete form, GenWeb allows you to search all known genealogical databases on the www.

Chapter 6

The Meaning of Community, Kinship, and Family

Remember Lisa's grandfather's story in Chapter 4, in which he—like many other young Swedes of his generation—was left behind when a parent emigrated to the United States. When he came to the United States to look for his mother, he did not find her, but he did become for a time part of her brother's household on a North Dakota farm. One aspect of the Scandinavian American experience is that the family composition varied according to circumstances.

As was the case with many other ethnic groups that helped to make up the great wave of European migration that began in the middle of the 1900s, Scandinavians who immigrated to the United States came primarily from rural farming communities. Often these farming families were large—it was not uncommon for them to include a dozen or more children—and entire households rarely immigrated together. Frequently, the male head of the household would precede the others by six months or so to establish himself and gain some means of supporting his family before he sent for them.

After 1890 the number of large family groups emigrating from Scandinavia declined markedly. The reason for this change in immigration patterns is not hard to find: By 1890 there was no more free land available in the United States under the Homestead Act. The vast majority of Scandinavians immigrating to the United States did so with the specific goal of becoming landowners. In mid- to late-nineteenth-century America, they were able to obtain large plots of land in the then-distant midwestern states

The majority of Scandinavian immigrants to the United States sought to become farmers. They brought to the isolated midwestern states high levels of literacy and industriousness.

and territories at prices even impoverished families could afford. These regions, rich in resources but comparatively unpopulated, needed the Scandinavians, with their industriousness, their high level of literacy, and their large families.

Although they assimilated rapidly into American society, Danes, Finns, Icelanders, Norwegians, and Swedes did tend to form ethnic enclaves. Social life for most such communities generally revolved around the Lutheran Church, which in Scandinavian countries had the status of a state religion. There were, of course, competing institutions. In Finnish American communities, for example, a schism often developed between those devoted to the church and those whose attention centered on consumer cooperatives, which were often aligned with radical political organizations. But publication of newspapers in their native languages (particularly important for the Finns, who had a greater burden to over-

Like other immigrant groups, Scandinavian Americans have maintained a strong sense of cultural identity while embracing their adopted country. Members of Swedish societies turned out in native Swedish dress for the dedication of Philadelphia's Swedish American Museum in 1938.

come in learning English) was a common feature of Scandinavian American communities and contributed to their cohesiveness.

By the 1980s, however, only four Finnish-language papers, with combined subscriptions of 2,000, survived. Perhaps no statistic is more telling of the success of Scandinavian assimilation into American society than this. By the third generation, it is clear, most Scandinavian Americans had lost fluency in the languages spoken by their immigrant ancestors. At the same time, marriages outside their original ethnic groups, migration to cities and suburbs, and the merger of distinctive Lutheran sects all contributed to a decline in ethnic awareness. Just as Scandinavian American kin groups have incorporated individuals of non-Scandinavian descent, kinship is by nature a broad and flexible concept. For example, single-parent families, adoptive families and foster families may all develop kinship bonds.

Tips for Adoptees

If you decide to pursue a search for your birth parents, it is very important to approach this project with sensitivity and caution. First, consult some of the books listed in the **Resources** section that deal with adoption searches. Talk with your adoptive family about why you want to study the history of your biological family. Think for yourself about your own goals for the project. Do you want to find information about your birth parents, or do you actually want to meet them? In most states, adoption records are sealed until the adoptee is eighteen years old. Your adoptive parents may know some basic facts about your birth parents that can help you gain a sense of that aspect of your heritage.

Your genealogical research need not include a search for your birth parents. It is entirely possible to investigate your Scandinavian American heritage without doing so, focusing instead on literature and history that details the experience of the particular ethnic group you know yourself to be a part of. If you are Norwegian American, for example, you will certainly want to read the epic works of Ole Edvart Rölvaag and Sigrid Undset described in the preceding chapter.

Alternatively, you could research the genealogy of your adoptive family—who themselves might be Scandinavian American. In a very real sense your adopted family has become your kin, and sharing this aspect of your family history will offer rewards to all of you.

Children of single-parent families may wonder whether there will be difficulties in conducting a genealogical search if they have limited contact with one side of their family. It is important to realize that many people exploring their Scandinavian American heritage—or any other ethnic background—know only one immigrant progenitor. Your present family structure will have little bearing on your study of your Scandinavian American ancestor. If you would like to know more about the family history of a parent with whom you do

Even renting a video of a Greta Garbo movie can be an opportunity to celebrate your Scandinavian American heritage. Garbo, Ingmar Bergman, Henrik Ibsen, and Hans Christian Andersen are just a few Scandinavians whose work is still enjoyed all over the world.

not live, be senstitive to the feelings of your other parent. Decide on a goal for your research, and discuss with your family whether it is realistic.

Celebrating Heritage

No matter what the composition of your family, there are endless possibilities for you to research your genealogy and Scandinavian heritage. Pick up a novel by a Scandinavian or Scandinavian American author. See a movie featuring the actress Greta Garbo. Spend an hour or two visiting an older relative, giving him or her the opportunity to speak about your family's fascinating past. You will come away from the experience enriched, with a greater knowledge of the people and events that shaped the history of the United States as well as your own personal history. Exploring just a fraction of the resources in this book will open up a world of discovery and celebration.

Resources

KINSHIP AND ADOPTION

Adamec, Christine, and Pierce, William L. *The Encyclopedia of Adoption*. New York: Facts on File, 1991.

The introduction provides a brief history of adoption. Entries explain key terms such as "adopted away/adopted in" (legal terminology referring to a child and his or her birth family and a child entering the adoptive family), organizations such as the American Adoption Congress, and a range of records and services. Many entries include bibliographies and addresses. The appendix also provides important addresses, statistics, and additional bibliography.

Askin, Jayne, with Molly Davis. *Search: A Handbook for Adoptees and Birthparents*, 2d ed. Phoenix, AZ: Oryx Press, 1992.

A detailed introduction to searching for birth parents, including chapters on the costs of searching; reference resources in government institutions, libraries, and genealogical societies; state and federal laws governing adoption; instructions on how to access primary data such as hospital and agency records, and records for black-market babies; alternative sources of information, such as newspaper and magazine ads; search and support groups; family reunion registries; hiring researchers and acquiring legal assistance; a reading list of adoption-related books and articles.

Bayer, Alan E. *The Assimilation of American Family Patterns by European Immigrants and Their Children*. New York: Arno Press, 1980.

Chapters on immigration laws, different immigrant groups (age, sex, marriage and family factors), occupational variation, differences in rural and urban settings. Contains many detailed tables of data.

Boatright, Mody C.; Downs, Robert B.; and Flanagan, John T. *The Family Saga and Other Phases of American Folklore.* **Urbana: University of Illinois Press, 1958.**

See especially Chapter 1, "The Family Saga as a Form of Folklore." Mody Boatright explores how and why families develop their own histories.

Bodnar, John. *The Transplanted: A History of Immigrants in Urban America.* **Bloomington: Indiana University Press, 1987.**

See chapter on "Families Enter America."

Brown, Gene, ed. *The Family.* **New York: Arno Press, 1979.**

A compilation of newspaper articles on the family from 1870 to the 1960s, emphasizing family relationships, changes in women's rights, the institution of marriage, the impact of the Depression, World War II, and changes in parental roles.

Dolgin, Janet L.; Kemnitzer, David S.; and Schneider, David M., eds. *Symbolic Anthropology: A Reader in the Study of Symbols and Meanings.* **New York: Columbia University Press, 1977.**

See Chapter 2, "Kinship, Nationality, and Religion in American Culture: Toward a Definition of Kinship."

Ehrlich, Henry. *A Time to Search.* **New York: Paddington Press, 1977.**

Chapters on searching adoption records, individual stories of adoptees, reunions with birth parents, an interview with adoptive parents.

Farber, Bernard, ed. *Kinship and Family Organization.* **New York: John Wiley, 1966.**

For the advanced reader interested in sociological theories of family structure and development. See especially the discussion in Chapter 1 of types of families.

Feigelman, William, and Silverman, Arnold R. *Chosen Children: New Patterns of Adoptive Relationships.* **New York: Praeger, 1983.**

Chapters on social factors, single-parent adoptions, the adoption search controversy, "adoptive parents' attitudes and adoptees' inquiring behavior."

Fisher, Florence. *The Search for Anna Fisher.* **New York: Arthur Fields Books, 1973.**

An account of an adopted child and her search for her parents. She describes her efforts to contact other adoptees and her meeting with her birth father. It is also a story of how the search affected her identity. Told in story form with gripping dialogue and dramatic scenes.

Gediman, Judith S., and Brown, Linda P. *BirthBond: Reunions Between Birthparents and Adoptees—What Happens After . . .* **Far Hills, NJ: New Horizon Press, 1989.**

Several stories of reunions between adoptees and birth parents, chapters on why reunions happen, what happens afterwards, and on birth fathers, siblings, birth mothers, and adoptive parents. Includes notes, bibliography, and adoption, reunion, and postreunion resources.

Gordon, Michael, ed. *The American Family in Social-Historical Perspective.* **New York: St. Martin's Press, 1973.**

An important introduction to the study of family history. Divided into five sections, each covering a different aspect of family and kinship.

Graburn, Nelson. *Readings in Kinship and Social Structure.* **New York: Harper & Row, 1971.**

The introduction is a clear explanation of the study of kinship. See also Chapter 4 on "The Genealogical Method," and Chapter 6, "American Kinship: A Cultural Account."

Hareven, Tamara K. *Family Time and Industrial Time: The Relationship between the Family and Work in a New England Industrial Community.* **New York: Cambridge University Press, 1982.**

Explores the interrelationship between three different kinds of time: individual time, family time, and industrial time. Hareven studies the interactions of individuals with the larger historical process.

Hvidt, Kristian. *Flight to America: The Social Background of 300,000 Danish Emigrants.* **New York: Academic Press, 1975.**

See Chapter 9, "Families or Individuals in Emigration?"

Hyde, Margaret O. *Foster Care and Adoption.* **New York: Franklin Watts, 1982.**

Includes bibliography and sources of further information, which lists several organizations such as "Adoptees in Search," "Adoptees Liberty Movement Association," "Orphan Voyage," and "Parent Finders."

Lasch, Christopher. *Haven in a Heartless World: The Family Besieged.* **New York: Basic Books, 1977.**

See Chapter 1 for a provocative discussion of the making of the modern family.

Lifton, Betty Jean. *Journey of the Adopted Self: A Quest for Wholeness.* **New York: Basic Books, 1994.**

An adopted child herself, Lifton has divided her book into three parts that mirror the phases of the adoptee's psychological development: "The Self in Crisis," "The Self in

Search," "The Self in Transformation." She includes a valuable resources section.

———. *Lost and Found: The Adoption Experience.* **New York: The Dial Press, 1979.**

Part 1 focuses on the psychology of the adoptee from childhood to adulthood. Part 2 concentrates on how adoptees decide to search for their birth parents, stages of the search, varieties of the reunion experience, what happens after the reunion, the roles of fathers, siblings, and wives of adoptees. Part 3 deals with the adoptee's relationship with adoptive parents. Includes information on adoptee search groups.

Livingston, Carole. *"Why Was I Adopted?"* New York: Carol Publishing Group, 1978.

Illustrated children's book that explains how and why children are adopted and attempts to answer many of the adoptee's basic questions.

Maxtone-Graham, Katrina. *An Adopted Woman.* New York: Remi Books, 1983.

The story of her search for her birth parents, beginning with the agency from which she was adopted. A detailed account of her court-ordered agency search, her reunion with her mother, her search for her father.

McGinnis, Thomas C., and Ginnegan, Dana G. *Open Family and Marriage: A Guide to Personal Growth.* St. Louis: C. V. Mosby Company, 1976.

See the early chapters for a useful discussion of family life in the early 1900s.

Mindel, Charles H.; Habenstein, Robert W.; and Wright, Roosevelt Jr., eds. *Ethnic Families in America: Patterns and Variations,* 3d ed. New York: Elsevier, 1988.

Immigrant families must often grapple with the tension between their native countries' traditions and American culture. This book examines the ways in which ethnic families adapt to life in the United States.

Modell, Judith. *Kinship with Strangers: Adoption and Interpretations of Kinship in American Culture.* Berkeley: University of California Press, 1994.

Chapters on the history of American adoption, birth parent experience of adoption, growing up adopted, the adoptee's search for a birth family, the birth parent's search for an adopted child, how the changes in adoption policy are affecting attitudes toward kinship. Includes an extensive bibliography.

Perin, Constance. *Belonging in America: Reading between the Lines.* Madison: University of Wisconsin Press, 1988.

A provocative exploration of the meaning of family and community, with sections on "drawing family lines," "converting friends to family," "parenting people," and "the constitution of men and women." Bibliography.

Pincus, Lily, and Dare, Christopher. *Secrets in the Family.* New York: Pantheon Books, 1978.

See especially the prologue, "Secrets in the Life Cycle of the Family," for a discussion of the myths that develop in a family, the relationship between these myths and the facts, and how these myths are carried from one generation to another.

Powledge, Fred. *So You're Adopted.* New York: Scribner's, 1982.

Chapters on how adoption has changed, the statistics of adoption, how the adopted child develops, the adult adoptee, searching for roots. Bibliography. A concise and clear introduction to the subject.

Rosenberg, Maxine B. *Being Adopted.* New York: Lothrop, Lee & Shepard Books, 1984.

An illustrated children's book about Rebecca and her life as an adopted child.

Sachdev, Paul. *Unlocking the Adoption Files*. Lexington, MA: Lexington Books, 1989.

A book about the "adoption rectangle—adoptive parents, birth mothers, adoptees, and social work personnel—and their attitudes toward opening adoption records." Chapters on the nature of the controversy, case studies of record releases to adoptees, birth mothers, birth fathers and siblings, registry and post-adoption services, and attitudes of social work personnel.

Schneider, David M. *American Kinship: A Cultural Account*. Englewood Cliffs, NJ: Prentice-Hall, 1968.

Discusses the way kinship is perceived culturally. See especially Chapters 2 and 3 on basic kinship terms for relatives and the family and how cultures modify them.

Shell, Marc. *Children of the Earth: Literature, Politics, and Nationhood*. New York: Oxford University Press, 1993.

A fascinating study of how different societies establish kinship and family. Recommended for advanced readers and for those wishing to take a very broad view of family history. Extensive notes and bibliography.

Skardal, Dorothy Burton. *The Divided Heart: Scandinavian Immigrant Experience through Literary Sources*. Lincoln: University of Nebraska Press, 1974.

See Chapter 7, "Change in Immigrant Values; Home and Family."

Thorne, Barrie, and Yalom, Marilyn, eds. *Rethinking the Family: Some Feminist Questions*. New York: Longman, 1982.

See the overview chapter. Somewhat difficult for nonscholars but helpful in thinking about new ways in which focusing on women redefines family life and history.

Weston, Kath. *Families We Chose: Lesbians, Gays, Kinship.* **New York: Columbia University Press, 1991.**

A study of gay and lesbian families, especially valuable for its numerous accounts of individual families, with anecdotes and narratives that provide models of how to tell the history of nontraditional families. Includes a statistical appendix on nontraditional families, extensive notes, and bibliography.

Wishard, Laurie, and Wishard, William R. *Adoption: The Grafted Tree.* **San Francisco: Cragmont Publications, 1979.**

See especially Part I; concentrates on the decision to seek out birth parents (where to get help, developing your choices and living with them). Other chapters on parents, the legal process, the adoptive family. Includes an appendix on adoption resources and glossary.

Conclusion

By now you realize that the story of the United States is the story of you and your immigrant family, writ large. By pursuing your own genealogy, you will be adding not just to your awareness of who you are and where you came from, but to the fund of knowledge that informs the American people of their collective past.

Pursuing your Scandinavian American ancestry is going to be a worthwhile and enjoyable endeavor. This book has suggested many different kinds of projects. You can be a historian, an autobiographer, an interviewer, a fiction writer, a photographer, a biographer. Each project represents a different point of view, another angle on your family's past. Each project develops different but complementary skills, encouraging you to try out different roles. The making of family trees, oral histories, and other kinds of albums of experience transforms you into an interpreter, analyst, and creator. The end product will convey your history to the world, claiming a place for your family as your own progenitors did in generations past.

Glossary

archives Organized body of records; a repository of evidence.

assimilation The immigrant's absorption into the prevailing or mainstream culture.

cooperatives Organizations or communities that organize around a common goal, often economic. A group of people agree to share resources on a nonprofit basis, usually selling goods or services to the public. Many Scandinavian Americans established such organizations.

Crimean War War for domination of southeastern Europe which lasted from 1854 to 1856. France, Great Britain, Turkey, and Sardinia defeated Russia.

data Information gathered for the purposes of analysis.

dissenters Those who disagree with commonly held opinions or who may protest the policies of a group such as a government or church.

emigrate To leave one country or region to settle in another.

family, extended Grandparents and other relatives such as aunts, uncles, and cousins.

family, nuclear The group comprising a mother, a father, and their children.

family tree Chart or diagram of family descent, showing how various branches are related to each other.

gender The classification of sex, male or female.

genealogy Record or table of descent showing how a family, group, or person is descended from an ancestor or ancestors; a lineage; the study of family histories.

genogram   A family tree that emphasizes both genealogical and psychological relationships as well as significant family events.

Homestead Act   An act of the U.S. Congress in 1862 that granted public land to any citizen or alien intending to become a citizen. The land, which was not to exceed 160 acres, was to be used as farmland.

immigrate   To enter and settle in a country or region of which one is not native.

imperialism   The extension of rule or influence by one government, nation, or society over another. Sweden, for example, dominated at various times the culture of its Scandinavian neighbors, and Russia has similarly encroached on Finland.

Kalmar Union   A unification of the kingdoms of Denmark, Sweden, and Norway. It was signed in Kalmar, Sweden, in 1397. The Union proved unstable because each of the three countries had elective rather than hereditary crowns. Sweden broke away in 1523. Norway and Denmark split in 1814.

kinship   The state of being related by common ancestry or a strong family bond.

neutrality   In international law, a nation that does not take sides in a war.

Nordic   Pertaining to the Germanic peoples of northern Europe and Scandinavia.

patrilineal   Denoting descent through the male line of ancestors.

patronymic   Adopting a modified form of the father's given name as a surname.

progenitor   A direct ancestor.

realism   Perspective in literature that attempts to describe life without romanticizing or idealizing it.

romanticism   A term applied most often to nineteenth- and twentieth-century literature, which was inspired by the French Revolution's emphasis on liberty and equality and on the intensity of the individual's experience, most especially that of great artists, who relied on their own inspiration rather than the traditions of literature (often called classicism).

Scandinavia The region encompassing the countries of Denmark, Finland, Iceland, Norway, and Sweden.

source A person, book, document—anything that supplies information.

Viking Pirates from the Scandinavian countries who plundered the coasts of Europe from the eighth to tenth centuries.

Index

ABOUT THE AUTHORS

Lisa Olson Paddock is a lawyer and free-lance writer. She has published books and essays on literature and the law. **Carl Sokolnicki Rollyson** is a Professor of English at Baruch College, The City University of New York. Both Carl and Lisa have traveled in Scandinavia and will be returning to Stockholm for a research project.

ILLUSTRATION CREDITS

Cover, © David De Lossy/The Image Bank; cover inset and pp. viii, 5, 6, 35, 37, 39, 41, 42, 44, 94, 96, 100, 116, 118, 128, 136, 149, 150, 152, BETTMANN. *Color insert*: pp. 2, 5, 9, 16, BETTMANN; pp. 3, 4, Courtesy of the Danish Tourist Board; pp. 6, 15, © AP/Wide World Photos; p. 7, © Lorentz Gullachsen; p. 8, © Möller; p. 10, Jan Butchofsky-Houser/Corbis; p. 11, Roger Ressmeyer/Corbis; p. 12, Macduff Everton/Corbis; p. 13, Charles Lenars/Corbis; p. 14, © Solvang Visitors Bureau.

LAYOUT AND DESIGN

Kim Sonsky